GOD IS ALIVE IN HOLLAND

God is Alive in Holland

Willem Jacobus Cardinal Eijk

with Andrea Galli

Gracewing

Dio vive in Olanda, first published in Italian in 2020 by Ares, Milano

Translated from the Italian by Vernon and Giulia King,
Translation Box, www.translationbox.com

First published in English in 2022 by
Gracewing
2 Southern Avenue
Leominster
Herefordshire HR6 0QF
United Kingdom
www.gracewing.co.uk

ISBN 978 085244 997 4

Typeset by Gracewing

Cover design by Bernardita Peña Hurtado

'When the Son of man comes,
will he find faith on earth?'
(Lk 18:8)

CONTENTS

Foreword

Saint Willibrord

W E'RE IN UTRECHT, one Sunday morning in the autumn. It's the fourth city in Holland by size, but perhaps the most important for quality of life and a warm welcoming vibe from the locals. Thousands of university students speed past on bikes, the tables of bars stand on the edge of the canals, almost touching the water. It breathes an air of Nordic respectability, not austere but rather friendly.

My wife and I were looking for a Mass in the city centre and we realised that the range of possibilities was much more limited than we had expected, and we were not expecting much. When we checked the times against distances on Google Maps, the suggestion that emerged was for the Church of Saint Willibrord at number 21 Minrebroederstraat, twenty minutes' walk away.

Willibrord, a harsh-sounding name to the Italian ear, practically unknown to Latin peoples, was the monk who, between the end of the seventh century and the beginning of the eighth, led the evangelisation of the Frisians, a Germanic people who lived in present-day Holland. He set out from Ireland, even if he was originally an Anglo-Saxon, was ordained a bishop, and established his episcopal see in the Roman *castrum* of Ultraiectum, that is, Utrecht.

We were surprised that the Mass that we had selected was celebrated according to the Extraordinary Form of the Roman rite: yet another reason for curiosity.

We quickly reached a little street where we had been the day before, a stone's throw away from the majestic Saint Martin's Cathedral, with its 112-metre-high bell-tower—the Madonnina in Milan Cathedral reaches 108 metres—that unfortunately fell into the hands of the Calvinists in 1580. The only problem was that we could not see any signs of a church in Minrebroederstraat. Unless you turned your head back a great deal and looked up. In this way it was possible to catch sight of a bell-tower that suddenly appeared out of the red-brick walls identical to those of the surrounding houses. Then you could see that there really was a church, moreover of a considerable size, but it had been built as if visitors and locals should not become aware of its presence. A camouflage that, as in the case of the nearby cathedral, made you think of the troubled presence of Catholicism in this land over the centuries.

In fact Willibrord was the first to realise that the Frisians were a hospitable but unstable people, capable of giving the Church great happiness, but also great grief: after a period of evangelisation that went very well, with many conversions, the pagan king Radbod reacted and, taking advantage of the death of the king of the Franks who had been protecting the missionaries, tried to eliminate the presence of Christianity and to revive the cult of the ancient gods. Willibrord was forced to flee, and his work was swept away. Only when Charles Martel restored order was he able to return. Although he was of an advanced age, he resumed preaching and christening. And what had seemed lost was gradually reborn.

We went in through the open door on the street and found ourselves in an atrium, where we caught sight of photographs of Pope Francis and of the Archbishop of Utrecht, Cardinal Willem Eijk. From the leaflets on display on a stand we realised that behind that Mass and the church itself was the Society of Saint Pius X: I smiled because the followers of Lefebvre were honouring not only Peter's successor, but also the local bishop, with a consideration that perhaps not all the local fraternities or religious societies displayed.

Once inside the church we knelt down, sat on the benches and looked around, while the organist was warming up on the keyboard. It was at that point that I realised that I was in a sacred building that, although almost invisible from the outside, on the inside hit you with the impact that masterpieces deliver.

It was a late-19th-century church, therefore relatively recent, built in a neogothic style that did not feel either artificial or forced. It gave off a golden splendour together with a sense of simplicity, of the devotion of humble people, with its lovely statues of the saints and of the Virgin Mary. The warm colours of the glazing and the columns devoid of human representations, with arabesques that could be found on the walls of a drawing room of the time, dispelled that sense of awe that the great height of the structure could give. At that moment I understood a comment that I had read on the Internet and which I had frankly considered an exaggeration: 'The most beautiful church in Holland'.

Whether this is, in fact, true or not I cannot say, but it is, undoubtedly, a church that conveys something of the former splendour and brilliance of Dutch Catholicism. It is a world that ought not to exist anymore if you just consider the bare numbers or the image that many people have, both inside and outside the Church. Instead, it is a world whose spirit seems to pulsate, like a flame in the dark, in that secluded temple dedicated to the apostle of the barbarous Frisians, among a few dozen people deep in prayer with their bilingual mass-book, some women with their heads covered and a number of young couples.

Incidentally, it gives cause for thought that this church is run by a community of priests that in the 70s, when it was founded, was seen by many as a product of the past that would melt away within a short time. This did not happen and that handful of priests, in the midst of difficulties and paradoxes, have held out and managed to assert their presence, unexpectedly, in the very heart of Utrecht, where, in the meantime, many congregations that seemed as strong and long-lasting as oak trees have collapsed.

But the authentic spirit of Dutch Catholicism is also found in other places. The faith that made Holland one of the main sources of missionaries in the world, up to the 60s, survives like an ember under the ashes. An ember that is burning. And it is on this subject that I wanted to talk to Cardinal Eijk, in an interview arranged for the day after.

The appointment was in the archbishop's residence, an unremarkable two-storey building in a residential district. Sharing tea and biscuits, this pastor, born in Duivendrecht, a village of 5,000 inhabitants on the outskirts of Amsterdam, on 22 June 1953, revealed hitherto unknown episodes of his life and, through the prism of his experience, talked about what it means to be a Catholic in Holland today. A conversation that we should have resumed in March, but which was postponed because of the pandemic, until the emergency passed also in hard-working Utrecht and in its surrounding areas. This is the final report of that meeting.

Andrea Galli

1

BLESSED ARE THE POOR

Your Eminence, let us start from basics, so to speak: let's talk money. Someone arriving in Holland from Germany notices instantly how different the resources and facilities of the Catholic Church are in these two countries, though they are so near each other and both economically advanced. You appear to be poor Christians in a rich country. Or am I exaggerating?

I CAN TELL YOU this. I took up my position as Archbishop of the Metropolitan Archdiocese of Utrecht on 26 January 2008. My previous diocese, Groningen, was a suffragan diocese with about 100,000 Catholics, whereas the archdiocese of Utrecht has over 700,000. Many saw my move from Groningen to Utrecht as a promotion, but in fact I suddenly became poor: for several years by that time the Archdiocese of Utrecht, which had once been really wealthy, had its finances in the red.

Even before I arrived, the treasurer had warned me that if I left everything as it was the Archdiocese would technically be bankrupt by July 2009. But in reality I did not have a year and a half to solve the problems. The previous diocesan staff, in fact, had approved an economic plan that would come into operation nine days after my arrival. It was a plan for making savings, but was nowhere near to what was needed to resolve the crisis. The first thing I had to do, therefore, was to cancel that plan, and within only a few days.

Having planned that operation, some weeks before my arrival in Utrecht I gave notice that I would straightaway appoint a vicar-general, the vice-rector of the seminary and a chancellor that I brought with me from Groningen. With their help and that of the treasurer, I drew up a more drastic plan to avoid bankruptcy.

It was not at all easy to accomplish. The curia, together with the pastoral centres of the deaneries, had 104 employees on the payroll. By the way, the work of these people was the responsibility of the management committees of the deaneries—which restricted the powers of the archbishop—although they were paid by the curia. In order to dismiss the staff I had, therefore, to abolish the deaneries, an action that did not go down well with the management committees. It was by no means an easy situation. We had to prevent one or more of the deaneries, which had a legal status in the Utrecht Archdiocese, from raising a legal challenge, as that would have resulted in a considerable delay in implementing the plan to save money, with the risk of making bankruptcy unavoidable. In the end I replaced five deaneries with three vicariates, run by episcopal vicars, directly nominated by me.

As a result of this difficult reorganisation, the personnel of the curia were reduced by two thirds. We tried to help everybody find other work, and we succeeded in this as well, except in case of two members of staff. It is important for me to stress that the union to which the majority of the employees of the curia belonged was very complimentary about the way the archdiocese had managed this transition and dealt with its workers.

Unfortunately, since we know that the money is bound to decrease further, we need, as far as possible, to shed further staff. Our funds come mainly from the contributions of the parishes to the overall finances of the curia, that is, 9% of their of their annual income. And given that the income of the parishes, mainly made up of voluntary contributions from the parishioners, are falling by 1–2%

each year, the curia is receiving less and less money. In Holland there is no *Kirchensteuer* [ecclesiastical tax] as there is in Germany or in Switzerland, nor is there a system like the 8‰ [voluntary contribution out of tax] in Italy. There is a clear-cut separation of Church and State. And since the numbers of churchgoers are falling, it is hardly surprising that the contributions also are decreasing. As a result, the parishes find it hard to pay for their staff and for the upkeep of their churches.

Certainly a system such as the *Kirchensteuer* would make life more comfortable. But, as it is, nobody can accuse you of accepting favours from the State.

Yes, this is one of the advantages of not receiving any funds whatsoever. The Church in Holland is free from any influence on the part of the State. It is free to set out and defend its position in the areas of medical ethics and matrimonial ethics; it is free to explain its social doctrine even when this comes into opposition with what politics and the laws of the State lay down. Without fear of pressure.

As soon as you arrived in Utrecht you had to 'cut to save'; what reactions did you have?

The drastic reorganisation of the Curia, inevitable to avoid bankruptcy, did nothing to help my public image, which was already marked by the fact that I was openly defending the teachings of the Church in the field of ethics, and I was trying to improve the liturgy in line with the directives from Rome.

I found myself described as a cold moderniser, a bishop interested only in money and not in pastoral care. However, I think I can say that proclaiming Christ and his gospel according to the teachings of the Church, improving the celebration of the liturgy and involving and widening the role of the deacons in the parishes, stressing the relationship of the diaconate with the Eucharist and prayer, are proofs of my pastoral commitment.

Furthermore, I dare say that shortage of money can seriously put the brake on pastoral initiatives. In the words of the old joke, when the Church cannot balance its finances, it can be futile to discuss which person should give the first or the second readings at Mass: they will both be read by the bailiff.

What is the financial situation today?

The curia is financially sound, but in the meantime the problem has shifted to the parishes. Between 2007 and 2011 more than 300 parishes have been merged to come down to 48 in number, but with the establishment of a parish dedicated to students in the city of Utrecht they became 49. Some of these parishes have as many as 13 churches. The reason behind the mergers is the loss of churchgoers, with the added difficulty of finding members for the pastoral councils.

However, even in these large parishes economic problems have started to occur. The number of paid employees has more than halved. In a note on the future of the archdiocese, published in November 2014, I wrote that in my opinion within ten years there would no longer be any paid staff, such as the lay pastoral assistants, except for the priest.

But, obviously, the priest cannot do everything on his own. So we have set up courses for training volunteers who are willing to serve as catechists or help the priests in other ways. These courses are attracting widespread interest, which is promising.

In any case, as I was saying, there is the growing problem of the church buildings. The parishes cannot afford to keep open all their churches, given that the costs of maintenance are too high. Some years ago a parish in a town in the archdiocese was forced to close, in a short period of time, six of its seven churches in order to avoid bankruptcy. Now there is only one church, large and beautiful, which is quite full for the Mass on Sunday and which has an excellent musical accompaniment to the liturgies (there are four choirs). This is an example of the concentration of resources.

In the note to which I referred earlier I had made another prediction, that is, that in 2028—the year when I am obliged to offer my resignation to the Holy Father according to canon law, as I will be 75—the archdiocese would have about 20 parishes with one or two churches in each. My hope is to have in the archdiocese a certain number of churches with active communities of the faithful around them. Possibly at that time the number of priests and churches will be balanced, so that it will be feasible to celebrate the Eucharist every Sunday in every church, something that is impossible at the moment.

Closing down a church where the Eucharist has been celebrated for decades, selling it off and seeing it turned into something secular, is more than unnatural for a Catholic. Does it have to be done?

Slowing down the closure of the churches carries the risk that the parishes may lose too much money, and future generations may be left empty-handed. Obviously it is a heavy responsibility to ensure that the deconsecrated churches have a new, worthy function, that they do not become churches of Satan or houses of prostitution. Some have been sold to communities of Eastern churches, but still Catholic, others to Protestant communities, at least remaining Christian churches.

The Dutch bishops forbid the sale of a church to be used as a mosque. Some have become medical centres, others have been converted to apartments. And in the sales contract the parish must insert a clause that forbids the new owner from reselling it to people who wish to use it for unethical purposes. In Holland this is called a 'chain clause'. This is effective in the short and medium terms, preventing the feelings of churchgoers from being hurt. But it does not work for ever.

The closures of churches and their loss to religious rites always are sad events for the faithful, for the pastoral councils, for the parish priest and his helpers, and also for me as a pastor, obviously. Several times every day in the archbishop's residence I walk past a portrait of one of my predecessors, Henricus van de Wetering, who was Archbishop of Utrecht from 1895 to 1929. In that period he consecrated over 100 churches. A century later I have the sad task of having to close down many of them.

This makes me sad. However, this also means building the Church of the future: it is already coming about and will consist of fewer buildings, but around them, as I said, there will be lively communities of the faithful.

What effect did the period of the pandemic have on you?

The pandemic has been a dark time for society and also for the Church. In Holland there is a clear separation between Church and State, and the latter may not interfere in the internal life of the former. Nevertheless, we are also part of a council that maintains permanent contacts between the Government and twenty-nine Christian Churches and two Jewish communities.

In March 2020 we made a voluntary decision to bring down to thirty the number of people present for the celebrations of the Eucharist. However, some of these events were found to be sources of contagion, with the result that we suspended public celebrations for some time. We have made decisions in line with the recommendations of the Government.

In this country, as in others, many parishes have transmitted live Masses online, and some were surprised to see that the number of individual contacts, on YouTube or other channels, was higher than the number of people who normally attended Mass.

As bishops, we asked for the churches to remain open so that people could access them to say a personal prayer, to light a candle and, above all, to worship Christ, and we asked for the Most Holy Sacrament to remain visible. From the following 1 June, theatres, cinemas, restaurants and bars got the green light from the Government to reopen, although with reduced numbers, and we too decided to do the same, and gradually increased the number of worshippers present at the Mass. Before that, we had invited the faithful to take a spiritual Communion when they followed the celebrations online, and on 14 June, the Sunday of the Feast of Corpus Christi, we restarted giving the Eucharist. And it should be noted that in the months before the faithful asked us many times to be able to take Communion.

So the period of the pandemic has been unprecedented, difficult, dark, but on the other hand there have been bright signs. We asked for expressions of solidarity, such as bringing food to redistribute to those in need—all of a sudden many people found themselves with financial problems as a result of the closure of many businesses—and the response was excellent. At the beginning of the coronavirus crisis I wrote in a message to the Catholic community that we were compelled to face up to an illness for which we had no treatment and no vaccine, and that gave us another chance to consider that we are in the hands of God, the Divine Providence. We hope that many people were able to reflect on the fundamental questions of life and started again to pray.

Who are the poor in Utrecht?

Before Covid the unemployment rate was 4%, but the lockdown was a heavy blow. The State did do something (but only for those who had a fixed employment contract), covering 90% of pay, over three months, when companies were not able to pay their employees, provided the company did not make them redundant. We invited people to come to church to pray but also to leave food for our charities, and many did so. The poor often do not talk about their own economic problems and from the outside they go unnoticed.

In every parish we have an organisation for the dea- conry, the charity, some flourishing, others less so, but they all provide help: food, clothing or other items for those in difficulty. And they are in contact with the local administrations, which often ask for help from our services or from those of the Protestant community. In the world of the deaconry we still have a strong presence, and most of the volunteers in Holland belong to a Church. The problem is that they are getting old.

In the Archdiocese of Utrecht there is a prize that is awarded to the best charitable project, and it is dedicated to the memory of Alfons Ariëns, a priest who was a major figure in the Catholic social movement of the twentieth century and the founder of the Catholic workers' union. When he was an assistant parish priest he was very active in caring for the workers of Enschede, a city in the east of the Archdiocese, where cloth and textiles were produced.

There was a lot of poverty and alcohol abuse, and he did everything he could to improve the conditions of the workers: personal development, with cultural activities, and religious education. The archbishop of the time did not fully understand why Ariëns was spending so much energy—he came from a farming family and perhaps was not fully aware of the specific difficulties of the working class –, but later he revised his opinion and came to admire that strange priest, giving him the title of monsignor.

Ariëns has provided an exemplary model . He prayed a great deal and said that the source of his charity was the Eucharist, underlining the relationship between liturgy and the diaconate. We are trying to do the same thing. We cannot celebrate the Eucharist in all the churches, but I have asked that in every parish there is one church where the Eucharist is always celebrated and that this particular church is the point of contact for the charitable activities. Because charity comes from a living relationship with Christ.

How is your typical day organised?

I get up at 5.30, have a shower, get dressed and go to the chapel. I start the day with a prayer to God and the offer of myself to the Immaculate Heart of Mary, in order to prepare myself for the sacrifice of the Mass, which I start celebrating between 6.00 and 6.15. After this I spend half an hour or so meditating on the day's readings, then say the breviary until Terce. At least, that's how it is at the moment: when the work of restoring the archbishop's residence is completed, I shall resume celebrating the Mass at 7.45, so people from outside can also take part.

After that I have breakfast and rapidly read two newspapers, in order to know what's happening in Holland and in the world. From 9.00 onwards I have appointments with parish priests, deacons and lay pastoral assistants. There are meetings with the presbyteral council, the chapter, the committee for the economic affairs of the archdiocese, and, once a month, the committee of the Episcopal Conference.

I am also the chancellor of the Utrecht Faculty of Theology, which is part of the University of Tilburg: I have to confer the *Missio canonica* on the Faculty lecturers after assessing their publications. Then I have meetings with the dean and sometimes with the board of management of the University.

I celebrate the Eucharist also in the parishes and sometimes in religious communities, alongside confirmations, on the occasion of jubilees or after the restoration of a church, for patron saints' days, but also for ordinary Sunday Masses, especially before a religious festival. Obviously I celebrate also in the cathedral for special occasions and for ordinations.

I have an apartment on the second floor of the archbishop's residence: I live alone, but during the day there are cleaning women and a cook to help. During the working day there are 20–25 people here in the archbishop's residence. Two auxiliary bishops live close by, on the other side of the garden and the car park.

Going back to my commitments, there are also pastoral visits to the parishes. They take up a lot of time, because I need to meet the parish priests, talk to members of the parish council, and so on, but they are important, they allow me to have an updated picture of the diocese and its state of health.

I receive a lot of letters; for some things I can get my secretary or my chancellor to send a reply, but there are also personal letters to which I have to give a response myself. Then there are letters that I have to write to the Roman Curia, to the papal nuncio, for instance, when I am asked to give my opinion on the election of a new bishop, matters that fall under the papal secrecy. I definitely receive far fewer telephone calls than in the past, because they have been replaced by e-mails: between 50 and 70 arrive every day.

At the end of the afternoon I take a walk, during which I pray the Rosary and before dinner the Vespers. If I am alone, I have dinner between 7.00 and 7.30. At the end of the day I go to the chapel, for 15–20 minutes, in front of the tabernacle, without anything to read, and I examine my conscience. I go to bed between 10.30 and 11.00.

Where does your faith come from?

My mother was a Catholic. After her baptism in 1921, her father, that is, my grandfather, whose name I was given, as they were returning from the church, said to my grandmother, 'This is the last baptism that we shall attend'. My grandmother, whom I got to know better after the death of my mother, was unable to explain the reason for his attitude. My grandfather had joined the Navy at a very young age—he had subsequently become a radio operator—when he was already a staunch socialist and soon afterwards he no longer wanted to go to Mass. My great-grandmother was a devout and practising Catholic, but my grandfather paid more attention to his father, also a socialist and a convinced atheist.

Both my grandfather's family, originally from Rotterdam, and my grandmother's family, from Amsterdam, belonged to a generation that fell into what was called the 'hidden trap for Catholics', because a quite significant number abandoned the Church in the first half of the last century, more or less between 1900 and 1940. A phenomenon that happened in silence in the large cities in the western part of the Netherlands.

My grandfather's name and therefore mine also, Willem Jacobus, that is, William James, shows that the family had strong Catholic roots. Our patron saints are Saint William of Vercelli and Saint James the Greater, a happy match. William of Vercelli (1085–1142), among other things, founded the Abbey of Montevergine, near Avellino, after making a pilgrimage to Santiago de Compostela, where indeed the tomb can be found of Saint James the Greater, the apostle and brother of Saint John, also apostle and evangelist. Jesus used to call the two brothers 'sons of thunder', which certainly gave some indication of their character, fiery, we might imagine. Saint James was the first apostle to become a martyr, executed by the sword during the persecution of the Christians in Jerusalem by King Herod Agrippa in the early 40s of the first century, as we read in chapter 12 of the *Acts of the Apostles*.

The name William, that is, Willem in Dutch, is derived from the German name Wilhelm, which means 'I want a helmet'. Both this name and the designation 'son of thunder' refer to fighting, being ready to fight. Since as a priest, as a moral theologian and as a bishop I have often had to fight to proclaim and defend the doctrine of the Church, I bear the name Willem Jacobus with pride, even though my grandfather from whom I inherited it rejected the faith. In my study I have a portrait of Saint James the Greater and one of Saint William of Vercelli, gifts from friends who were priests, Italians, and several times every day I ask for their intercession to enable me to follow their example, at least to a small degree.

My father on the other hand was a Baptist, but he abandoned his faith after the Second World War. As a Baptist he was against the baptism of children: he himself was not baptised until he was 18 years old, in 1937, in the Baptist church in Purmerend, 15 kilometres north of

Amsterdam. On that occasion the Baptist community gave him a Bible, of which he was always very fond, even after he stopped going to church. I still have it in my bookcase.

The attitude of the Baptists towards baptism had a consequence: my father did not want my sister and me to be baptised. However, as we know, in a family, when the women really want something, they win ... and so it was with my mother. When the time came for my sister to start primary school, my mother saw her opportunity. Very close to where we lived there was a Catholic primary school belonging to the parish, run by a community of nuns, with a fair number of pupils and with one teacher for each class. Two kilometres away there was another primary school, but with fewer pupils and, above all, with one teacher taking more than one class. Making a big deal of these factors and how the Catholic school had advantages, my mother was able to influence my father on the choice. This led also to another fact: it was necessary to baptise the children. And so my sister at the age of five and myself at six months old were baptised together. It was 22 December 1953, just before Christmas. My sister still has memories of our baptism.

This explains the good that Catholic schools can do, even in the earliest classes.

Yes, also because the primary school also had a nursery school, which had a decisive role in my discovery of the Catholic faith. The ways of the Lord are truly unfathomable, as Saint Paul says in the Epistle to the Romans (Rm 11:33). Divine Providence had prepared my vocation as a priest by means of a complicated route.

It was in the autumn of 1958 or in the spring of 1959, at any rate during the last year of nursery school. On a very sunny day we went to visit the parish church, across the road. It was the first time I went into a church. This church, which, by the way, was quite pretty, had been built in 1878. It made a strong and unforgettable impression on me, although I understood almost nothing, since my family never went to church. I remember also that some children gave a kiss to the statues of the guardian angels that supported the pulpit, almost furtively, when the teacher and the priest were not looking: it was symbolic of a society where people still believed passionately in guardian angels.

In my first year of primary school, my mother, who had got to know the priests in the parish, started to go to Mass every Sunday with my sister and me.

In the same year I received preparation for my first Communion from a lady teacher, a lay person, who had been teaching for almost 40 years. This lady, who was deeply religious and had a severe face, introduced me for the first time to Jesus. She passed on to me a fire, lighting faith in my heart. Although I was only six years old, when I received my first Communion on 26 May 1960, after making my first confession, I knew very well that with the Eucharist I was receiving Jesus himself, his very body.

I remember the date exactly, also because I was given a small plaque as a souvenir of what remains one of the greatest events in my life: it is hanging up in my apartment, in the archbishop's residence, and I pass it several times a day, I see it very often.

I received very clear instruction on Heaven, on Hell and on Purgatory. The fire that the Holy Spirit lit in me through this lady has never gone out, whereas many in my class, although they heard the same things, lost their faith in the course of a decade with the arrival of affluence and of a culture of self-interest in which everybody felt he was Pope of himself. In my case the fire of faith has never gone out and has resisted many attempts to smother it, unfortunately even on the part of a number of priests.

And when were you confirmed?

In March 1963, after being prepared by a schoolmistress in the fourth year of primary school, whose faith was, if possible, even stronger than the teacher that had prepared me for my first Communion. During the celebrations when I received this sacrament, I heard the organ of our parish church for the first time. My mother used to take my sister and me to Mass early on Sunday morning, when there was no singing as in the High Mass. For this reason, the sound of the organ was new to me, and it stole my heart: in that moment I was certain, I had to learn to play the organ.

I had to keep asking my parents, because musical instruments and lessons were rather expensive at that time. However in the end it was possible to buy a piano, and a Protestant organist that lived in our village taught me to play both the piano and the organ. He was a person of faith and had a good knowledge of the Catholic liturgy and its music. He taught me to play with passion. He also taught me in a Reformed Church in Amsterdam, where there was an impressive organ, with three keyboards, which had a great impression on me as a child.

Unfortunately, in the Amsterdam of the 80s that had become atheist, the church was closed and the organ was split up and sold in three parts. I became the organist of my village church in September 1970 and kept the position until the beginning of 1980, when I entered the seminary.

But also in the seminary I played the organ, often accompanying Mass and Vespers and some ordinations of priests in Roermond Cathedral. I frequently played for liturgical events also when I was a lecturer in the seminary. But my studies of medicine and of medical ethics, and my

specialisation in moral theology, then my pastoral commitment as priest and then bishop, gradually left me no
time to play.

**You mentioned the seminary: when did you first think
of becoming a priest?**

From the time of my first Communion I felt a certain
desire to become a priest, a spark, but it became a flame
one day when I was playing with a school friend in the
garden of his house. At some point his mother called him
to come into the house. There in the lounge sat the
assistant parish priest, who was looking for new altar boys
and had come to ask if my friend was available. However,
he was not sure. I don't know if his parents had detected
something in me, perhaps they had become aware of my
particular interest in the Church, as I often used to talk
about it.

My parents too were rather surprised by this, but they
were not unduly worried. At any rate, since my friend was
hesitating, while the priest was pressing the point, the parents
decided to call me, so that the invitation to become an altar
boy could be addressed to me as well. I was very surprised,
but I immediately agreed with great enthusiasm. I thought
that my friend's parents had rather expected that ...

At that point my friend also couldn't say no, but he was
never a passionate altar boy, whereas I was. I went to serve
at Mass with enthusiasm. I was often given the first Mass
on working days: I never missed it and I enjoyed getting
up early. I often spoke of this commitment and of the little
things to do with the church, because it was an important
matter for me, and inevitably we talk a lot of the things
that we carry in our hearts. I remember that one Saturday
afternoon, at a scout meeting, I told another boy perhaps

three or four times that I had to serve at Mass the following day, until he burst out with 'I know!'

One day I was visiting my paternal grandmother. She asked what I had planned to do when I grew up. I gave a forceful answer: 'I want to become a priest!' My father became very angry and shouted, 'This will never happen! Are you mad?' However, my grandmother, who was a practising Baptist believer, warmly defended me and said to my father, 'Are you mad? He is the one who has to decide what he should become'. I am still grateful to her for her words, which made my father shut up. It was a powerful and a painful episode. From that moment an embarrassed silence fell on the subject, but my desire to become a priest did not wane. From that time onwards I did not open up much to my parents, even on other subjects.

A very serious test that my vocation had to overcome occurred at the high school. It was a Catholic school and there were still a number of teachers who were priests, who belonged to a religious congregation. In the first two years the level of religious education was still good, but from the third year, 1967–68, the hours devoted to religion changed and lost any religious content. And I'm talking of lessons with priests. There were discussions about everything, from politics to abortion and free love, and there we could smoke in class. It had already happened after I came to the high school that there were priests that left the ministry but nevertheless continued to teach. This is what used to happen: at the beginning of the school year there was a simple communication that such and such a teacher should no longer be called 'father' but 'sir'.

Let's say that this was not the ideal atmosphere to nurture a vocation as a priest. I remember that in the first year almost all of my fellow pupils went to church every Sunday. At the end of high school there were only two of

us. In Amsterdam, and also in our village which was close
by, you could plainly see the drop in practising Catholics,
looking at the benches in the church Sunday after Sunday.

Just before I left school I asked the headmaster for
information on studying theology at the Catholic University of Nijmegen and at the Faculty of Catholic Theology
in Amsterdam. However, in the end my choice was
determined by another painful experience. In the last two
years of high school my mother was suffering from a
tumour. She was in considerable pain in her abdomen, but
she never complained, never even talked about it. She lived
her illness in silence. She died two months before I took
my final school exams. While I was going to visit her in
hospital, my thoughts turned to study medicine and I
opted for that route, at the University of Amsterdam,
putting my vocation as a priest 'on hold'.

**'On hold' in the sense that the idea was to go to
university first, and then to enter the seminary?**

Let's say that that I very much enjoyed my medical studies,
which I started and finished with enthusiasm. But the
desire to become a priest was still there. The last year
before graduation I was made a very attractive proposal
that I could not refuse: the professor of internal medicine
offered me a post in his department, which would enable
me to become a doctor of internal medicine. I accepted
and was later admitted to the specialist course that would
last five years.

At that point, however, I found myself at a crossroads,
which set me thinking: stop, it is the moment to decide
what to do, become a priest or a doctor. The person who
helped me understand what was truly my path, what God
wanted for my life, was my parish priest, in the parish
where I was born and raised, at Duivendrecht, a village, as

I said, next to Amsterdam, and, incidentally, very close to the stadium of Ajax, at that time a football team admired and famous all over the world.

What gave me the Catholic faith and made me a disciple of Our Lord was not my family but the parish, starting from the primary school. All the priests that I saw passing through the parish, despite their faults and their human weaknesses, had a strong faith. They celebrated the Mass with devotion, I saw them reciting the breviary as they walked in church or in the garden of the vicarage. Every one of them in his own way was a good model for a boy thinking about the priesthood.

In the month of August 1969, and so at the height of the tensions, of the polarisations and of the chaos that beset the Dutch Church, it was a new parish priest, Fr George Laan, who, together with his housekeeper, greatly helped me to strengthen my vocation. He asked me to become the organist, and we gradually became friends. During the vacations I was able to live in the rectory, because I no longer had the possibility of going home, since my father did not agree with my decision to follow my vocation as a priest.

In order to take the decisive step and choose between seminary and medical specialisation, he advised me to go on a spiritual retreat for one week in a monastery, under the guidance of a Jesuit father. It was the first time I came across the methods and education of the Jesuits, which I later experienced also in the seminary where I studied.

At the end of the week of exercises I could not ignore the fact that I had a special calling from Our Lord and had to say yes. I say, 'had to', but in reality I could no longer resist the desire to become a priest. God reveals the vocation to the priesthood or to a religious life through a

strong, undeniable urge to follow Him in a life of consecration. He did this with me, too.

I therefore decided to leave the hospital of Amsterdam
University, where I was working in the department of
internal medicine. I was unable to resign immediately, and
so I entered the seminary a few months late in January 1980.
Again following the advice of my parish priest and of the
Jesuit with whom I had undertaken the spiritual exercises,
I chose for my training as a priest, and for the study of
philosophy and theology, the seminary of Rolduc in the
diocese of Roermond, founded by Bishop Johannes Gijsen
in 1972. At that time it was the only seminary still left in
Holland that was organised, let us say, along traditional
lines. I was ordained deacon on 15 September 1984, in
memory of the Blessed Virgin of the Sorrows, and became
a priest on 1 June 1985, the day of Saint Justin Martyr.

Fr George Laan came to the conclusion that my life as
a priest would be marked by many afflictions and difficulties. At the time I did not pay much attention to those
words, but later I would understand them better.

**Holland has been the scene of a bioethical revolution
before other countries in Europe. How did you as a
Catholic and a doctor live through those events?**

The bioethical revolution started in Holland in 1969 with
the publication of a pamphlet, *Medische macht en
medische ethiek* ['Medical power and medical ethics'] by
Jan Hendrik van den Berg, a professor of psychiatry at the
University of Leiden, who advocated ending the life of
children born with severe physical problems, especially as
regards limbs, caused by thalidomide—also known as
Immunoprin, Contergan or Softenon—, a drug popular at
the end of the 50s and the beginning of the 60s, which was
used by pregnant women to combat nausea.

Although Van den Berg was talking of an act that did not also envisage that adults would ask to die, his book triggered a very intense debate also on the possibility of acceding to the request for death on the part of a sentient person. The most striking fact was that we were at the end of the 60s, but in the discussions it was evident that the idea that human life had an intrinsic value, regardless of its condition, had already been dropped: everything revolved around the issue of whether or not society accepted a life of suffering: in fact, we were already firmly convinced by the ethics of autonomy.

How was it that this rapid collapse took place in Holland of all places?

A fascinating question. Up to the beginning of the 60s Holland was, at least on the surface, one of the most Christian countries in Europe, yet at the end of that decade it became the trailblazer for euthanasia and assisted suicide. It is certain that the growth of the economy in the first part of the 60s contributed to the growth of a hyper-individualistic culture, which turned into secularisation and acceptance of an ethics of autonomy, where man has the absolute right to do what he wants with own life.

This culture has been so pervasive that even the Churches have been strongly affected. At the end of the 70s euthanasia and assisted suicide were already virtually accepted. I had direct experience of this when, after my medical degree, I started to specialise in internal medicine in one of the hospitals that at the time was part of Amsterdam University. One day, while talking with other doctors and nurses about my position on the value of human life, based on the Fifth Commandment 'You shall not kill', and my rejection of euthanasia, I found myself isolated. Nobody was on my side. The professor of internal medicine was against euthanasia, but only because he was afraid of the judicial consequences since it was not yet legal.

I remember going over a number of questions and objections: since the administration of pain killers can sometimes, as a collateral effect, hasten death, and since this can happen also as a result of refusing the use of means to prolong life, should we not admit that actively putting an end to life, by the administration of lethal doses of medication, can also be morally acceptable? Is it not inhuman to compel people with incurable illnesses to continue to suffer? And if life is a gift of God, is it not possible for a human being, who is seriously suffering, to return this gift to the Creator?

Since I did not know how best to answer these complex questions, I decided to write a dissertation on euthanasia for the Faculty of Medicine of Leiden University. This was also a response to a request which my bishop had made, while I was still studying in the seminary, to examine in depth medical ethics. But even while I was studying medicine, I had sensed the difficulties I would meet in this area as a doctor. In my fifth year at university (1975–76), one of the two professors of obstetrics and gynaecology said during a lesson that the clinic where he operated did not accept as candidates for specialising in gynaecology people who refused to carry out abortions. He recommended that those who had such convictions and wanted to become gynaecologists should apply to the Catholic hospital in Amsterdam. Adding, however, that there were no longer many students left with these views ...

I must say, in fact, that, apart from myself, I only remember one other student on the course who was opposed to abortion. It was in that Catholic hospital, which later dropped the epithet Catholic, that I received my medical training at the end of my studies: today abortions are carried out there as well, in cases where it has been established, by means of prenatal diagnosis, that the baby in the womb has an illness or handicap.

As an assistant doctor I twice came across a request for euthanasia. The first time was at the beginning of my career, in the Department of General Internal Medicine. I said to the woman who asked for euthanasia that my religious convictions prevented me from doing that. I told the chief physician what had happened, but he said nothing to me. I learnt later that he himself had carried out euthanasia on that woman. Perhaps he was afraid that I could report it to the police or the judiciary, even if by then there was in practice immunity for those accused of that crime.

There was also a Catholic man, suffering from an incurable tumour in his lungs, who asked me for euthanasia, when I was an assistant doctor in the department of pulmonary diseases. After explaining to him my opposition to euthanasia, I encouraged him to trust in the possibilities that medicine could offer him in the natural terminal phase of his illness. In addition, I urged him to give thought also to his faith, to his being a Catholic, and I suggested that he should search for the strength to face his suffering in prayer and in the sacraments. The man followed my advice and called for a priest to give him the last rites, and he died in peace shortly afterwards. The chief physician, who had heard positive words about me also from the relatives of the patient, showed his appreciation for what I had done.

This case taught me that as Catholics, not only ordained but also lay, we have to be more daring and speak of the strength the Lord give to sufferers through prayer, the sacraments and spiritual assistance.

There is an objection that you mentioned earlier which also involves faith: if our life is a gift from God, why can we not give it back to our Giver, thanking Him for his generosity but saying 'Now is enough'?

Because ending life on our own initiative means rejecting this precious gift and is, therefore, a sign of ingratitude. Certainly we can and we must give our life back to God, but in a completely different way, by imitating Jesus, who accepted suffering and death on the cross. We can give our life back to God by joining Jesus in his sacrifice. Together with Him we find the necessary strength to carry our cross and discover the meaning of life when life suffers pain. We can offer the sacrifice of ourselves for the purposes that we have in our heart, for our fellow man in difficulty or in danger.

This assimilation of our suffering with Christ's suffering, this union of ourselves with His suffering finds its supreme fulfilment in celebrating the Eucharist, with the sacrifice on the cross that recurs in a bloodless but real way. The food we swallow is digested and transformed into the substances that make up our body. But in receiving the Eucharist the opposite happens: we are transformed into the Eucharistic food, that is, into Christ, whereby our sacrifice becomes one with His. Because of the current crisis of faith many undervalue the strength of the grace that we receive in the sacraments and that makes possible what is impossible for us, but not for God.

God has given us life in a particular way: we have been created in His image. And man is made up of soul and body, not just soul and not just body. Human beings have been created in their totality in the image of God. God and those who have been created in His image are never merely a means to an end. This involves both the soul and the human body. To sacrifice the corporeal life in order to eliminate suffering means downgrading the life to a simple means, which violates its essential value.

In the case of euthanasia also there is talk of the law of the slippery slope. How did you see this happen in Holland?

In the 70s and the early 80s many were fighting for the legalisation of euthanasia in the terminal stage of a physical illness, saying that there would be only a few cases. Many others, including the Dutch bishops, warned that it would not be like that. They were right. Later on came acceptance of the termination of life even before the terminal phase of a physical illness, and in the 90s also in cases of mental illnesses, in cases of dementia and of new-born babies with handicaps.

Whoever accepts the termination of life for a certain degree of suffering will always find himself faced with the question whether the same cannot apply to a slightly lower level of suffering. It is easy for the door, once a little ajar, to then become wide open.

The Dutch government that was in office before the present one had stated in 2016 that it wanted to arrive at a law that allowed a person to ask for assisted suicide even in the absence of illness, but when there was only suffering linked to factors such as loneliness. When we make ourselves masters of life and death, even to a small degree, we are creating a culture of death of which John Paul II had warned us in his encyclical *Evangelium vitae*. All of this has gradually undermined the awareness of the value of human life in Holland. The Dutch media give little prominence to developments in this field. In the case of the 2004 Groningen Protocol, on the possibility of terminating the life of babies born disabled, the population, by then familiar with a large number of new cases of euthanasia, largely shrugged their shoulders. On the other hand, the foreign media spoke and wrote for days and days on this subject.

The Groningen Protocol was an agreement between paediatricians—especially one that was also a lawyer—from the department of neonatology in Groningen University Hospital and the public prosecutor of the city. The agreement laid down that a paediatrician who ended the life of a severely disabled new-born baby, having followed a series of precautionary measures, would not be prosecuted. The Protocol was particularly concerned with new-borns affected by serious handicaps who did not need intensive therapies and at the time of birth were not in pain, but who, it was to be expected, would suffer later in life. The paediatrician/lawyer mentioned above then published a list of 22 cases in which the Protocol had been applied: all cases of new-born babies affected by spina bifida but without further complications.

A neurosurgeon from the University of Rotterdam, who was not a Catholic, strongly criticised this list and the Protocol itself, saying that a person with spina bifida could live very well. At my suggestion, the Pontifical Academy for Life invited him to speak about the Protocol during one of its plenary sessions. In 2007 this Protocol had become legal across the country; at first it did not allow for the ending of the life of disabled new-borns who would suffer later on, but then, after a modification, it included this possibility. There were also many adults affected with *spina bifida* who protested against the Protocol. One woman in particular said in a television programme, 'If the Protocol had existed and had been applied when I was born, I would not be here today. But I love my life and find that it is very meaningful.'

From 2004, when people abroad started to talk a lot about the Protocol, whenever I introduced myself as

Bishop of Groningen, for example in Rome when I took part in the work of the Pontifical Academy for Life or in other conferences, almost always the reaction was 'Ah, the Groningen Protocol ...' Then I hastened to say, 'Yes, but I am not responsible for it!'

On one occasion the paediatrician/lawyer mentioned above, the public prosecutor of Groningen involved in the Protocol and I took part in a symposium on this subject that had been organised by an association of Protestant students, Calvinists. The symposium as such went well, but I was disappointed that the students present wavered between the acceptance of the intrinsic value of human life—such that we do not have the right to deal with life and death as we want, and even in the case of a new-born we must think of adequate palliative cures, as I highlighted in my contribution—and, on the other hand, the issue of the suffering of the new-born stressed by the paediatrician/lawyer. At that moment I perceived the first signs of a weakening of religious convictions among young Protestants of the most intransigent tendency, a weakening that over time has become ever clearer.

In the 70s, 80s and 90s there was not yet any law on euthanasia and assisted suicide. There was one case of euthanasia that reached the court, but the judge acquitted the doctor who had explained his choice as a case of *force majeure*, in the sense that he had to choose between two duties: on one hand to protect the life of the patient and on the other to relieve his suffering. The judge ruled that because the latter duty could only be achieved by ending the life of the patient, the actions of the doctor were precisely due to *force majeure* and he was not guilty. An argument that subsequently became the basis of the law on euthanasia.

What is striking is the fact that in Holland the debate on the introduction of euthanasia took place before the debate on the decriminalisation of abortion, in contrast to what happened in practically every other country, where the debate on abortion took place before that on euthanasia. The reason is probably that in our country the discussion on euthanasia started with the booklet of Van den Berg in 1969.

The decriminalisation of abortion carried out in certain circumstances was sanctioned by the law of 1981, but did not come into force until 1984.

The law on euthanasia applied in 2002, as in Belgium, whereas in Luxemburg next door it applied in 2009. As we feared, other countries have followed the example of Holland. In 2016 it was approved in Canada, and in the same year the bishops of that country invited me to speak on the subject.

The Dutch Episcopal Conference published a communique on 23 April 2020 about a case of euthanasia that divided public opinion. What was it about exactly?

In 2016 a female doctor in a nursing home had carried out euthanasia on a woman who had written a declaration in which she stated that she wanted euthanasia one day, in the eventuality that she ended up in a nursing home, as in fact happened. The declaration had been signed four years earlier. Back in 2002 the legislature had ruled that a written declaration for euthanasia had the same authority as a request expressed verbally, but had given no indication of the length of its validity. A declaration remains valid even if signed many years earlier. Except that the woman in question had written that euthanasia should be carried out only when she gave the go-ahead. But after she had been admitted to the nursing home she had lost the ability to express that intention because of the onset of dementia.

Despite this lack of clarity, therefore, the doctor decided—after consulting the family of the woman and two other doctors—to carry out the euthanasia. They maintained that the woman's suffering was unbearable and without any hope of improvement. But when the doctor tried to give the lethal injection, the woman, repeatedly, withdrew her arm.

The question then arose: was this gesture to be considered a refusal or not? In the end the doctor put a sedative in the old woman's coffee, so that she could administer the drug, and euthanasia was carried out.

However, the board of public prosecutors started legal proceedings against the doctor. In September 2018 the Lower Court cleared her of the charge of applying the law on euthanasia in an improper way. The case then proceeded directly to the Supreme Court, which in April last year also acquitted the doctor. The Supreme Court based its decision on the testimony of an anaesthetist, who explained that the movement of the woman in withdrawing her arm while the doctor tried to give the injection was not a sign of conscious resistance, but a simple muscular reflex, without awareness.

As you can understand, this is a verdict that leaves room for many arbitrary decisions affecting people with dementia, and not only them.

What are the profound changes of feelings in a society once euthanasia becomes legalised?

It is important to realise that the acceptance of euthanasia and abortion implies the acceptance of the possibility, broader and more drastic, of making decisions on human life, that is, on the line between life and death. Accepting this means accepting in broad terms all the other ways of dealing with the human body, for example, dealing with biological sexuality, as in the case of transgender people.

In the 90s a university clinic in Amsterdam developed programmes to reassign biological sex—the sexual organs and secondary sexual characteristics, such as the growth or removal of breasts, the stimulation or the repression of the growth of the beard, the pitch of the voice—in transsexuals, people convinced that they are living in the wrong body, men who want to be women and vice versa. The hormonal treatments and the operations necessary to reassign the biological sex—all paid for by the national health service—result in sterilisation, because the possibility of passing on human life is removed. This intervention on the human body is close to another intervention, the most dramatic, that on the boundary between life and death.

But let us think of certain types of 'enhancement', of improvement. According to some people, within twenty years it will be possible to connect people to computers by means of a chip in the brain, in the section responsible for memory. Improving the body by the modification of DNA is already possible in Holland in the form of so-called gene doping, the insertion into certain bodily tissues of a gene that is responsible for the production of a hormone, so that this hormone is produced in greater quantities without the need for injections or pills. The Catholic Church takes a positive view of the development of science and technology, if the medical interventions are for therapeutic purposes, if the body, and hence the person, is the objective of the interventions, but not if they demean the body or when the characteristics sought are an end in themselves.

Another way of intervening on the body is the use of procedures which replace sexual intercourse in the trans-mission of life, with the result that people become the product of a technique rather than the fruit of the love of their parents, love of which the sexual act—in a married couple—is the authentic expression at a physical level. Furthermore, by appropriating procreation we lose sight more and more of the fact that life, including that of children, is in the last analysis a gift from God and not something that can be imposed on nature. On the other hand, operations that help the sexual act to reach its natural goal, procreation, but are not a substitute for it, are legitimate.

In Holland since 2002 a law has made experiments also on human embryos possible, those that are left over after the processes of in vitro fertilisation. In 2016 the government legalised also the creation of human embryos to be used for research, currently only for experiments in the field of reproductive techniques. And given that today the majority of the population—including also Catholics and Protestants—take for granted the fact that human life, both before and after birth, can be manipulated at will, those Catholics that follow the doctrine of the Church in this matter are put under pressure.

You have explained how in medical circles there was already pressure in the 70s, I imagine today …

I can add some examples. The medical foundation that I set up, together with some friends, in 1993 has organised conferences and published a series of books on various aspects of bioethics and, in 2010, a manual of medical ethics in Dutch, also published in English in 2014. Some years ago this foundation wanted to create an association of doctors, nurses and obstetricians that followed the doctrine of the Church, but many of those who were in a position to join the association explained that they did not feel up to it.

The reason is that they did not want to be publicly identified, for fear of repercussions in the workplace. A hospital looking for staff would have immediately rejected their CV. The most they were willing to do was to be part of a network of professionals that was informal and not public. Genuine Catholics in a secularised country are in a very difficult position: they must be careful in order to find a job and then hold on to it. In a way we are already faced with a persecution.

I too have been subjected to vehement objections when, following my nomination as bishop of Groningen, it became known that in the seminary I had taught moral theology following the teachings of the Church, especially as far as homosexuality was concerned. And I suffered attacks within the Church itself when I spoke of other ethical subjects.

Once, during a meeting on euthanasia, as part of a theology course, when I spoke of suffering received and accepted in union with Christ, two people ridiculed this aspect of the teachings of John Paul II, who a few years later would give personal evidence of the Christian perspective on pain and of his teaching.

On another occasion, when I was called to a parish to explain the position of the Church on artificial insemination, I was met with an indignant reaction of the parishioners, who openly rejected the teaching. At the end of the evening some elderly women, perhaps wishing to mitigate that experience by showing me kindness and understanding, said to me, 'We're very sorry, but, you know, wherever you go and say these things you'll find a negative reaction'. I did not find those words very comforting.

2

'LEX ORANDI'

**Dutch Catholicism: a glorious history until the Second
Vatican Council, then a very sudden, dramatic crisis.
Like an athlete struck down by a heart attack. Can you
explain how this happened?**

YES. Immediately after the end of the Second
Vatican Council there was an incredibly rapid
collapse of the Dutch Church. From 1965 to 1975
the number of the faithful who went to Mass on Sundays
halved. After 1975 the trend slowed down but did not go
into reverse. An entire generation of young people left the
Church in the space of a few years and did not pass on
their faith to their children, except in a few cases.

The current situation is, therefore, the result of choices
made fifty years ago. Holland is considered one of the most
secularised countries in Europe. In 2016 31% of the Dutch
said they belonged to a Church or profess a faith, whereas
in 2002 there were still 43%. The number of official
Catholics, that is, those registered as such, dropped from
5,106,000 in 2000 to 3,882,000 in 2015, a fall of 24%. Two
churches close down every week, whether Catholic or
Protestant. Catholics going to Mass on Sundays numbered
385,000 in 2003, but 186,000 in 2015, a drop of 52%. In the
same period 269 churches closed out of the 1,782 that
existed in 2003. The trend is continuing: less than 50% of
Catholics have their children baptised.

The fall of the Dutch Church can teach us something
of interest on the causes of a crisis of faith never seen

before taken in terms of extent. Let's try to go back to the
40s of the last century. On 9 October 1947, to be accurate,
a group of nine people, both lay and priests, assembled in
the smaller seminary of the Archdiocese of Utrecht to
discuss some disturbing changes that they had observed
among Catholics across the country.

The results of that meeting were published in a book
with an appropriate title, *Onrust in de Zielzorg*, that is,
ferment in the care of souls. These people acknowledged
that there was a weariness in pastoral care, and also saw
that the link between Catholics and the Church was no
longer based on the contents of the faith, but had become
a sort of social relationship. Faith was seen as a set of
commandments and a system of abstract truths that did
not affect daily life. Belonging to the Church essentially
meant being part of a community: you went to the Catholic primary school, then to the Catholic middle school,
you were a member of Catholic associations, especially in
the fields of sport and scouting. You were Catholic because
of social connections, because you grew up in Catholic
circles, and not as a result of living a faith.

The group that met in Utrecht in 1947 had foreseen
very clearly the collapse that took place in the second half
of the 60s. One of them wrote on the subject of the
Catholics of that time: 'They are powerful armies that are
preparing for the great apostasy of the near future, a slow
and unseen process'. An important witness of this process
was also Karol Wojtyła. While he was studying for his
university dissertation in philosophy at the Catholic
University of Louvain, he made a visit to the Netherlands.
He wrote in a letter that he admired the solid organisation
of the Dutch Church and its activities, but at the same time
he noticed a spiritual poverty among the people and the
absence of a life of prayer, while the main emphasis was

on doing. He also wrote that the Church in Holland displayed a 'unity that was rather cold and hard', in contrast to the Protestant world, as if the desires, the needs, the religious feelings of churchgoers mattered very little: 'the only thing that matters is to experience unity'.

His successor in the papacy, Benedict XVI, also made similar observations when he visited Germany in 2011. I will cite one: 'In Germany the Church is organised in an excellent way. But behind the structures, can one find the same spiritual strength, the strength of the faith in the living God? We must say sincerely that there is an excess of structures compared to the Spirit. I must add: the true crisis in the Church in the West is a crisis of faith. If we cannot achieve a true renewal of the faith, all the structural reforms will be ineffective'.

A very solid exterior structure but emptied from within, like a tree with a hollow trunk that falls when the storm comes. It is a situation that also calls to mind what happened in Quebec or in Ireland? Do you not agree?

Perhaps. It is certain that the Dutch Church, with its unity based on social links more than on true faith, could not withstand cultural changes as radical as those in the 60s. In that decade per capita wealth grew rapidly, and this enabled people to live autonomously and therefore independently from one another. It was a great push towards that culture of individualism that later became hyper-individualism.

According to the Canadian philosopher Charles Taylor, this culture implies that the individual has not only the right, but also the obligation to differentiate himself from others, choosing his own religion, his own philosophy of life and his own range of values. Obviously that individual fails to understand that in making these choices he is influenced by the prevailing public opinion, by the mass media, by social networks, by the world of publicity. The result is that we are seeing the acceptance of a strict conformity, especially among the young. Anybody who has the courage to have ideas that differ from the prevailing public opinion clashes with the system.

This happens to those who want to be openly and truly Catholic. In this individualist culture each person stands on a stage and sees the others as spectators. The hyper-individualist does not accept anything that transcends him, such as the family, the State, the Church or God. And if he displays the need for one of these entities, it is a need for utilitarian purposes, that is for self-interest—normally economic—that the individual cannot achieve by himself, with his own resources. In this climate one cannot conceive of belonging to a community, such as the Church, that has shared convictions, even less can one accept having above oneself a Pope or a hierarchy that teach the beliefs of faith, including moral beliefs, guided by the Holy Spirit and sharing the authority of Christ.

Of course the crisis of faith has multiple causes. Even the idea that faith is incompatible with natural sciences has certainly had an impact. However, this idea already existed in the nineteenth century, when there were no signs of crisis among the majority of Catholics. This is an idea that was given a new impetus from the 70s of the last century by the computer revolution. However, here too we must recognise that the mass desertion of Catholics started earlier. In the 60s the content of the faith was no longer the cement that bonded Dutch Catholics to their Church. The ties that remained were loosened as a result of individualistic culture.

What are the lessons we can draw from these events, especially for those that are not Dutch?

In my view, there are at least three.

The first: a catechesis that simply passes on a collection of abstract truths and commandments, which do not affect daily life, do not help in the formation of a real Christian faith. Because a presumed faith that does not touch daily life loses its meaning. We must offer people a spiritual catechesis, that is, one which, besides passing on the truth of the faith and its related ethics, teaches living a life guided by the Holy Spirit, a life of prayer, a personal relationship with Jesus. This must be the guiding principle in the preparation of children for the First Communion, of young people for Confirmation, of couples for Marriage, and also in the guidance after marriage, and so on.

The second lesson: the catechesis, as well as being spiritual, must be unambiguous. As far back as the 50s priests, teachers and catechists, aiming to hang on as much as possible to the young people who wanted to leave, used to add, as you might say, water to the wine, that is, they diluted, they softened the message of the Gospels, especially in those aspects that could not be explained with pure reason. I heard from a witness, for example, that a Franciscan father, a teacher of religion in a high school in the 50s, used to tell his pupils who did not believe that Jesus really could have multiplied the loaves, as we are told in the Gospels, 'Naturally Jesus was not a magician; He had not really multiplied the five loaves and two fishes in order to feed a mass of thousands of men, but with His message of charity towards His neighbours, He convinced those present to share their bread with those who had not brought any'. This interpretation in reality has been heard elsewhere as well, with a number of variants, an indication that it was not the fruit of the creative mind of a single man of the Church, but something widespread at the time. Thus the Franciscan in question will have satisfied without doubt the sceptics who listened to him, but, at the same time, through the authority as a priest that he could still command at that time, he will have damaged the faith of the true believers in front of him.

Experience teaches us a third lesson: that the highest number of true believers, let's call them like that, are found in the parishes, which, even during the revolutionary storm of the 60s and 70s, maintained a truly Catholic character in their way of celebrating the liturgy. And this shows us the profound truth of the words '*lex orandi, lex credendi*', that is, the law of prayer is in line with the law of belief. Furthermore, these parishes have maintained also a good catechesis, in the sense that I said. All this has often depended on the presence over a long period of time, even decades, of a good parish priest, both brave and orthodox, like Fr George Laan in the parish where I was born. Today young people or families of believers, who do not find in their own parish a liturgy celebrated with dignity or a good catechesis, look for them elsewhere. The young are not concerned with the physical boundaries of the parish where they live, but look around them until they find a suitable environment.

So, there are three points, of which I want to stress the first two: a catechesis that is both spiritual and unambiguous, that is faithful to the Holy Scriptures, to the Tradition and the magisterium of the Church.

The Gospel is for all. Jesus, before he ascended to Heaven, told the Apostles, 'Go, therefore, make disciples of all nations; baptise them in the name of the Father and of the Son and of the Holy Spirit, and teach them to observe all the commands I gave you. And look, I am with you always; yes, to the end of time' (Mt 28:19–20). However, before we undertake this task, we must put our own house in order. I mean that we must do something to combat the unfortunate lack of knowledge of the faith and the doctrinal confusion that reigns among those Catholics that are still active and faithful. It is only after healing our own communities—at least in the West—that it will be possible to do something productive for the evangelisation of non-Christians and the re-evangelisation of those who were Christians in the past.

On the path to evangelisation there is contrary evidence that risks killing every effort. What impact did the scandal of sexual abuse committed by priests and monks have on the Dutch Church?

It is often thought that the scandal of the sexual abuses of minors by clerics and monks was one of the reasons that caused many people to leave the Church. I would, however, say that this is not the case in Holland. Here the number of Catholics and, above all, attendance at Sunday Mass had dropped long before, with the result that, on the contrary, it is almost amazing that the scandal had such a small impact on the number of registered Catholics and the number of churchgoers, given the shocking publications and articles that followed one another in the media.

However, this is not to deny that the abuses of minors that have come to light have damaged the credibility of the Church. These crimes are always abominable, but all the more so when they are committed by clerics and monks. If we consider the victims, but also the parents who entrusted their children to the care of priests and monks in the confidence that the parishes, the seminaries and the colleges were safe places, we can readily understand the gravity of what has happened. Also when we think that, alongside the perpetrators, there were bishops or religious superiors that tried to cover up those atrocities, perhaps moving the guilty elsewhere without punishing them.

The Dutch Episcopal Conference and the Dutch Religious Conference took a series of steps in the interests of the victims and provided a series of measures to prevent these tragedies recurring in the future. In the first place, in 2010 they set up a commission, called the Deetman Commission after the name of its president, to carry out an independent inquiry into the abuses committed against minors between 1945 and 2010. The Episcopal Conference implemented all the recommendations made by the Commission. For example, the creation of an independent foundation (the Foundation for the prevention and handling of sexual abuse in the Roman Catholic Church in the Netherlands), which is based on four pillars: a centre where complaints can be made, an independent commission to investigate such complaints, a commission to decide upon possible compensation, and a structure to assist complainants.

The bishops of Holland took these decisions of their own volition, not because they were forced by a law, by the government or by a tribunal. There was also the possibility to present complaints regarding acts committed by people now dead. The number of cases of sexual abuse examined was about 2,000, and the highest compensation paid was 100,000 euro. In all of this process bishops and superiors of religious orders collaborated closely with one another. When at a certain point the complaints seemed to have petered out, it was decided that the last day for presenting them was 1 May 2015. This applied to cases that were outside the deadline or that concerned people no longer alive. Therefore on 1 May 2014 the Episcopal Conference, together with the Religious Conference, set up a centre for people to report actions that exceeded the limits established in a code of behaviour in a pastoral context. Information about sexual abuse of minors is always passed on to the police.

Other measures have been taken: before a priest is ordained or a lay person is nominated for a pastoral post that involves minors, the person in question must present a declaration issued by the State that certifies that he has no criminal record. In addition, a diocesan priest, before starting to work in another diocese, must present a declaration from the bishop that certifies that there have been no problems of this kind in the past. This also applies to monks that accept an appointment in a diocese: they must provide the same declaration from their provincial or general superior.

Furthermore, seminaries offer special programmes to make future priests aware of the problem of the sexual abuse of minors. We do the same in the training of permanent deacons and lay pastoral workers.

In the light of all of this, apart from some publications that maintain a harsh and critical stance, I must say that there has been widespread appreciation of what the Dutch Church has done in relation to the cases of abuse that have come to light and of what it is continuing to do to prevent them. In 2017 the Dutch Minister of Justice and Security pointed out to the Jehovah's Witnesses, who are today facing many accusations of abuse and violence in their ranks, that the Catholic Church and the measures that it had adopted were a model to follow.

The history of Holland has been marked by conflict between Catholicism and Calvinism. Today in various countries that had experienced similar divisions we see the creation of alliances between denominations that were once hostile to each other, in defence of the heritage of Christianity in society. What is your experience?

In our country as early as the end of the nineteenth century the Catholic political party and the Protestant one understood that they had to co-operate if they wanted to achieve a majority in Parliament able to block liberals and socialists in the fight over Christian schools. The question was resolved in 1917 with a modification of the Constitution that established that Catholic and Protestant schools would be subsidised by the State in the same way as non-denominational state schools.

Catholics and Protestants were able to maintain a majority in Parliament until 1967. In 1980 the Catholic party and two Protestant parties merged to form Christen-Democratisch Appel (CDA)—Christian Democratic Appeal—which in the 80s more than once was the largest party, with around a third of the seats in Parliament. This, however, did not prevent Parliament from passing the law on abortion in 1981. Christian Democratic Appeal became secularised and very rapidly lost its original characteristics. It was a Minister of Justice of this party who, in 1993, introduced to Parliament a provisional regulation according to which a doctor would not be punished for assisting suicide or euthanasia, provided that he followed a series of measures and reported everything to a municipal coroner.

Besides this party, let us call it 'Christian Democratic', which is the biggest, there are two smaller Protestant parties, the Christen-Unie (CU)—Christian Union—and the Staatkundig Gereformeerde Partij (SGP)—State Reformed Party. Both have as one of their founding texts, apart from the Bible, the *Heidelberg Catechism* of 1563, which states that the Catholic Mass 'is none other than a negation of the unique sacrifice and the passion of Jesus Christ and is an accursed idolatry'.

For some years now the CU has given this catechism a less central place among its fundamental writings, in the hope of also attracting Catholic voters, and it did have some success. The SGP keeps the *Heidelberg Catechism* as one of its distinguishing elements. Many who vote for the SGP believe in the Calvinist doctrine of predestination, which teaches that, before He created the world, God decided who would go to Heaven and who to Hell after death, and that man is not able to change this destiny through moral actions, however good he is.

In 2017 the leader of this party endorsed the Nashville Declaration, which was signed by more than 150 Evangelical pastors and scholars, to reaffirm the Biblical version of sexuality and marriage.

Today the CDA has 19 seats in Parliament, the CU 5 and the SGP 3. In other words, the Christian political parties today have only 27 seats out of 150. That does not alter the fact that they still have considerable political influence. Currently the Netherlands has a government that is made up of a right-wing liberal party, a left-wing liberal party— the proponent of the 2002 law on euthanasia and of the 2001 legalisation for the so-called marriage between people of the same sex—and also the CDA and the CU.

These last two Christian parties are hindering the plan of the previous government to pass a law on the so-called 'fulfilled life' to allow the assisted suicide of people who say that they are suffering unbearably and without hope for non-medical reasons, such as being lonely, having lost a person dear to them or being of advanced age. The idea is that the individuals concerned can legitimately consider that their life is fulfilled, that is, it has come to an end, for the reasons given above, and that it makes no sense to continue it. This bill is the reflection of the exasperated individualism of Dutch society: an assistant, so to speak, not a doctor, would have the task of checking that the desire to end life by the person concerned is enduring and sincere, without any external pressure; if he is convinced that the person in question really wishes to die, he can provide him with the drugs to do so. It is not the role of the assistant to the suicide to assess whether or not the life is really 'fulfilled': only the would-be suicide can do this.

That said, although the liberals in the government declared that they were in favour of this legislative proposal, the two Christian parties were able to block it. This is a result of the collaboration between the Catholic and the Protestant politicians.

Is there also Catholic-Protestant co-operation on the ground? I'm thinking of hospitals and pro-life activities in general.

In 1972 Catholic and Protestant doctors, together with some atheists, founded the Nederlands Artsen Verbond (NAV)—the Association of Dutch Doctors. Its aim was to block legalisation of abortion and, later on, euthanasia.

At the start NAV had more than 2,000 members, mostly of a rather advanced age. But then the elderly members died and were not replaced by younger people, with the result that the numbers are dangerously low. An investigation in 2005 indicated that only 15% of Dutch doctors were against carrying out euthanasia or giving assistance to a suicide. After the law on abortion had been approved in 1981 and that on euthanasia in 2002 the opponents lost courage.

'What can we still fight against?', a member of the management committee of the NAV said to me at the end of the 90s. Catholic and Protestant jurists together founded the Juristen Vereniging pro Vita (JPV)—the Pro-Life Association of Jurists. NAV and JPV used to publish a fine journal on questions of medical ethics, but later, because of the falling numbers of subscribers, it became an online journal, appearing ever more infrequently.

However, this does not alter the fact that the collaboration between Catholics and Protestants in politics, which started at the end of the 19th century, is still worth maintaining, given the results that I have already mentioned.

Today there are more registered Catholics than Protestants. However, the percentage of those going to Church on Sunday is, on the whole, higher among Protestants than Catholics.

The explanation for this fact is that the Protestants, who in the past made up the vast majority of the population—I am speaking of the large Dutch Reformed Church (Nederlands Herwormde Kerk)—suffered a crisis long before us. Those that remain are often the most convinced and active believers. Furthermore, the non-practising Protestants tend to have themselves removed from the official lists, whereas the Catholics do not.

Most of the Protestants, as, unfortunately, most of the Catholics as well, have quite liberal ideas concerning abortion and euthanasia. A small percentage, the most strictly observant Protestants, who normally vote for CU or SCP, do not practice abortion or euthanasia. Many of them believe in the literal meaning of the Holy Scriptures. Nevertheless, the young among them, through watching television and using social media, come face-to-face with modern critical thinking and the positions of liberal Protestant pastors, and are beginning to feel ill at ease with a too literal approach to the Bible.

The fundamental principle of Protestantism is *sola scriptura*, that is, the belief that the Holy Scriptures are the only source of faith. Once this belief wavers, then the rest also starts to stagger. And today we are seeing a weakening of the faith and strong signs of secularisation even among the small remainder of Protestants that in theory continue to be strict believers. If this trend continues, it will certainly create difficulties for collaboration between these Protestants—who at the moment share many aspects of our social beliefs, of our medical ethics and of our moral standpoint on marriage and sex—and the Catholics.

We know that all of this has a smaller impact on the Catholic world, in the sense that for the Catholic Church the Holy Scriptures are the primary source of the faith. Nevertheless, the Bible does not give a complete explanation, because in some aspects different interpretations are possible. Therefore, we need also to turn to other sources of the faith, such as the Tradition of the Church and the documents of its magisterium, in first place those of the Pope, Christ's vicar on earth, guided to the highest degree by the Holy Spirit, and also those of the bishops in communion with the Pope. For this reason, an historical and critical interpretation of the Bible, if applied in conformity with the Tradition of the Church and the enduring teachings of the magisterium, cannot throw the faith into crisis.

We must not forget that there are also differences between the Catholic position and that of the strict Protestants, who are, in fact, Calvinists, particularly as regards the use of contraception and artificial insemination.

In 1993, together with an emeritus professor of anaesthesiology at the University of Maastricht, I created the Foundation for Medical Ethics (De Stichting Medische

Ethiek), in whose constitution it says that Catholic doctrine is the starting point for its activities, that is, organising symposia and courses, as well as publishing books and
articles on bioethical subjects. Since 2015 the foundation
has become the Catholic Foundation for Medical Ethics
(Katholieke Stichting Medische Ethiek), which gave rise
to the Network of Catholic Medical Professionals
(Netwerk Katholieke Zorgprofessionals). Protestants as
well can take part in its activities, such as symposia, but
they cannot become members of the Network, in order to
keep its make-up clear.

**Let's talk about the question of immigration: how does
the Church deal with this in Holland?**

Many people are worried about Islamic immigration in
Holland, because of the threat of terrorists or radicalised
Muslims entering the country. It is, above all, the right-
wing parties that emphasise this. However, we need to
remember that there are many Christians among the
immigrants. There are no firm statistics, but according to
an influential name in statistical science, Hans C. van
Houwelingen, in 2018 there were approximately one
million Christian immigrants living in Holland, both
coming from the West and from other places.

The diocese of Rotterdam estimates that the percentage
of Catholic immigrants or descendants of immigrants is
about 20%. The parish where I was born, in a village
bordering on Amsterdam, in the diocese of Haarlem-
Amsterdam, today consists of more than 60% immigrants.

The immigrants go to church more than the Dutch and
are more active in helping. They are often shocked by the
secularisation they see in this Europe, from where their
Christian faith came in the past, either directly or not, and
the way in which secularisation was able to penetrate the

Churches themselves. In their eyes there is a lack of any spiritual life in the Dutch Churches, the same thing that Father Wojtyła found when he visited our country in 1947.

In Utrecht the Mass with the greatest number of participants, including many immigrant families with small children, is the one celebrated in English in the Church of Saint Augustine, which, because of the renovations going on, has been moved to the Cathedral on Sunday afternoons. Many parishes in the big cities, especially Amsterdam, the Hague and Rotterdam, have been saved by the presence of a large number of immigrants.

It must be said that for the Dutch Church this influx of Catholic immigrants has been enriching, with a positive influence on the local churchgoers. In our parish churches Mass is often celebrated in a foreign language, and many of worshippers are studying or working in the University of Utrecht or the University of Agrarian Sciences at Wageningen. Then there are parishes especially for migrants, for example, the Vietnamese parish and the Polish parish, or the parishes for people of Churches with their own Oriental rite, such as the Syriac Catholic parish or that for the Chaldeans.

Contrary to what many people think, the number of Islamic immigrants is more or less equal to the number of Christian immigrants. In 2006 the percentage of Muslims in the total population of Holland was about 5%, that is, about 850,000 people. According to a report in 2018 the Muslims now are probably slightly more than 6%, about one million. In our country as well there are radicalised Muslims, who are quite young, but they are relatively few in number.

This is not to hide that, in spite of this, we have suffered from acts of terrorism. On the morning of 18 March 2019 in Utrecht a Turkish Muslim killed four passengers on a tram with a firearm and wounded others, some seriously.

It was a dramatic day for the whole population. The mayor had urged people not to leave home, except in cases of emergency, until the assailant had been captured. I published a message on the website of the archdiocese to express our condolences for the victims and our solidarity with their families, as well as with the actual witnesses of the attack and their relatives. It became known that the police and the secret services had managed to foil other attacks that had been planned by Islamic terrorists.

The Dutch Episcopal Conference has a commission for inter-religious dialogue, which meets regularly also with representatives of the Islamic world, in discussions that are calm and pleasant. The main problem with dialogue with Muslims is that they do not have a central authority.

It is a fact that also in Holland there are many that are afraid that immigration threatens Dutch culture and values, and for this reason two populist parties, the Freedom Party (PUV) of Geert Wilders and the Forum for Democracy of Thierry Baudet now have together 22 seats in Parliament. If, however, the question is asked about the nature of these values and about the specific aspect of Dutch culture, people are stunned and often cannot give a sensible reply. The authentic Christian culture of Holland has been radically undermined by the individualist culture of recent decades.

I should say, however, that the subject of immigration has a smaller impact in Holland than in Italy. Probably because in recent years there has not been such a massive inflow of immigrants as in your country; furthermore, Italy has economic problems and a level of unemployment that is disturbing, especially among the young. So I can imagine what position many Italians take on the subject of immigration, especially given the lack of solidarity shown by other member states of the European Union.

We need to do everything possible to save those who risk drowning at sea, to offer them a bed, food and the necessary sanitary conditions. In the case of those who have suffered discrimination and persecution in their own country, sometimes even risking being killed, we must give them all the protection they need, if necessary even in terms of a permanent residence permit. This form of solidarity is vital to uphold the dignity of all human beings, which creates an essential bond between us. However, a country is not obliged to give residence permits to those many migrants who leave their own country merely for economic reasons, in other words, in order to find the possibility of a higher income in a wealthy country. Their first duty is being able to contribute above all to the common good of their own country. Richer countries, however, which are often to blame for the destabilisation of poor countries, must give their assistance for the development of poor economies.

The economic situation in Holland is different from that in Italy. For example, unemployment is very low: at the beginning of 2018 there were about 380,000 people looking for work, who had not yet found it, that is, 4.2% of the active population. The fear that immigrants might take jobs that should go to the Dutch is very small. If anything, many companies have great problems finding qualified workers. From this point of view those immigrants that have professional qualifications and can speak Dutch reasonably well are very welcome.

In the collective imagination Holland is often associated with the easy consumption of soft drugs. How is this reflected in the life of the country?

Holland is tolerant as regards the use of *cannabis*, which can be bought in a coffee shop, but its production is prohibited: a policy that we can define as ambiguous and even hypocritical.

For a long time there has been a stream of people coming to Holland to buy *cannabis*. The mantra has always been: cannabis is a soft drug, less dangerous than alcohol, with acceptable side-effects. Gradually we are discovering that this is not true, that the young who use cannabis perform less well at school and many leave school without a certificate, which hinders them for the rest of their life. And it is not easy for them to stop the habit.

Furthermore there is no doubt that soft drugs open the way to using other drugs, because the need to anaesthetise the consciousness becomes ever stronger. Nowadays many use *ecstasy*, including even lawyers and academics, during parties at the weekend, and there are many labs in Holland that produce it. Many of these places are turning to the production of *crystal meth*, which is more profitable than *ecstasy* and is more dangerous as a drug, leading to addiction even after a single use.

Even Mexican drug-traffickers get their supplies in Holland. The fact that Holland is a country that has always been wedded to trade, and therefore very open—Amsterdam is an airport hub of major importance, Rotterdam is the largest port in Europe—the fact that it has a coastline that is long in comparison to the size of the country and very indented, the fact that one can easily travel from Holland to other key countries, all of this, together with a certain tolerance towards the use of drugs, has made it relatively easy to exploit Holland for the international trade in drugs and for their production.

At one time the undercover labs were hidden in farms, isolated areas of the countryside, but now they are found even in residential districts, this is clear from the waste that is left. At one time this problem was widespread mainly in the province of North Brabant, but now it extends to the whole country.

Returning to the earlier point, de-Christianisation: how have you managed to keep your faith? How have you engaged with the people that you have met in a barren or hostile environment?

I have always lived openly as a Catholic, firstly as a lay person and then as a priest and a bishop. During my medical studies at Amsterdam University, I used to pray before and after meals, in public, and cross myself. I was the only one still doing that. Every so often I was aware of some smiles of commiseration, but I continued to do so because I wanted to acknowledge Jesus openly.

In the last period of study, during my internship in the department of internal medicine, the doctor who was with me heard me say that I would never practice euthanasia, and said to me, 'So you are a convinced Catholic. And you're also against abortion, correct?'. I answered yes and said that I would never help with an abortion. 'And if it were your sister, if she was pregnant but did not want the baby, would you still be against abortion?'. 'Certainly', I replied. My attitude was treated by the doctor and the other students who were present as incomprehensible and reprehensible. 'You want your neighbour, even a member of your family to suffer!'

I was completely isolated in defending my position. I remember that shortly afterwards I was alone in the assistants' room together with a female student. She looked at me, and, shaking her head, said, 'Going to Church … no-one does it anymore!' Another time also a friend of mine, who was Jewish in origin, said to me, 'You are too rigid in your principles! If you happen to be with us, your colleagues, at some conference, and if in the evening we want to let our hair down, you will never be one of us. Accepting you in our circles will be difficult'.

Despite this, that is, despite being known to everybody as a practising, convinced Catholic, even labelled as a conservative, I was offered a job in the department of internal medicine of the hospital, shortly before the end of my studies, with the possibility of becoming a doctor of internal medicine. It was a test, because I was also considering becoming a priest. It was a temptation. But the desire that the Lord had put in my heart, as a sign of my vocation, was too strong. And so, after a period of prayer, after a number of spiritual retreats under the guidance of the Jesuit father that I have mentioned, I decided to resign from the university hospital, in 1979, and to enter the seminary in the diocese of Roermond—my own diocese was Haarlem—which was the only one to have maintained a traditional approach.

This was the moment when you took your vocation 'off hold', to use your earlier expression. What was the reaction of your family?

When my father heard of my decision he got very angry. For him this meant not only throwing away the possibility of a good career, but also to do so in order to carry out a ministry that, as a Protestant, he could not understand. My maternal grandmother also considered it a stupid decision.

None of my family was present at my ordination as a deacon nor as a priest. My father did not want to speak to me for three years. Afterwards, gradually, our relationship improved, and when I was nominated a bishop he was even proud of me, although, unfortunately, because of the state of his health, he was unable to attend my consecration as bishop.

What was your early life as a priest like, what were your first posts?

I was immediately made the deputy parish priest still within the diocese of Roermond. I had to give catechesis in three classes of the parochial primary schools, schools that by then were Catholic in name only.

In Holland the Protestant, Catholic, Islamic and other schools are financed by the State, but have their own management committees, whereas state schools are managed by the municipality. In the Catholic schools the teachers are baptised but often not only do not go to church but also know nothing about the Catholic faith. And *nemo dat quod non habet*, no-one can give what he does not have.

Whether or not a school does still convey something of the meaning of the word 'Catholic' depends on the attitude of the headmaster and the management committee. There are headmasters who, when talking to parents who have come to get information because they would like to enrol their children at that school, in order to reassure them, say, 'Don't worry, the fact that this school is Catholic will not cause you any problems!' The Catholic school is, consequently, a world in which, strange as it may seem, the priest often has to fight to affirm his presence as a ... 'Catholic'.

Nowadays most parishes no longer teach the catechesis in schools, especially in preparation for the First Communion and the Confirmation, because the schools make this task too difficult. But when I began my ministry in the parish, deputy parish priests, above all, were required to teach in a school.

In one of these primary schools the teaching team wanted me to use a method for the catechesis in which God was never mentioned even once. If I had not agreed, they simply would not have let me teach. When I understood the situation, I decided to act. I went to see the members of the management committee, to introduce myself and develop a relationship with them: I wanted them to get to know me before they started discussing amongst themselves the problem that I was about to unleash. After this round of introductions I informed the teaching team that I did not agree with the type of course that was proposed. When they told me that, as things stood, I would have to give up the post, I replied that the matter should be submitted to the management committee. And clearly the team had not realised that I had prepared the ground and had chances that they were not aware of.

In order to present the Gospel in schools that are nominally Catholic, but are, in fact, as secularised as the rest of society, it is necessary to put into practice what Jesus recommended: 'So be wise as serpents and innocent as doves' (Mt 10:16).

My parish priest too was a member of the management committee and he supported me, even if at the time he was only able to help me a little, as he was in hospital following an accident to his spine. We reached a compromise: before the lesson I was required to give a summary of what I would be saying to the teacher of the class where I was going to teach the catechesis.

To be on the safe side, I asked the then episcopal vicar responsible for the catechesis and the schools in the diocese of Roermond what he thought of that solution. He said that I done the right thing and, in time, I would gain greater freedom. And he was right. The resistance to the catechesis was coming from the teaching team, not from the pupils. The exception was in one school where there were many children of Muslim parents. They had to remain in the classroom even during the hours of religious instruction, and showed quite openly their dislike of the Christian faith.

On yet another occasion when I was deputy parish priest, I had to prepare a young pregnant woman, who was already living with her Catholic fiancé, for Baptism, Confirmation and First Communion, in readiness for Marriage in church.

I went to their home and asked if I could teach these catecheses in the presence of them both, as it would be a good preparation for marriage. The young man, who had recently come out of prison, assured me that in his case it would not be necessary. They had a dog, as tall as a man, with a fierce appearance, which was wandering around the room all the time, barking at everybody with its jaw wide open, showing its sharp teeth. With the eyes of that animal on me, I was trying to explain the elementary truths of the Christian faith.

At a certain point I remember that I raised my voice, trying to outdo the dog, and I asked the woman if she knew who Jesus was. She looked at me with a face that meant, 'What do I know?' She was saved from embarrassment by her future husband, who was passing through at that moment and said, 'Ah, I know who Jesus is; he's that man that burst out of the cave at Easter!' After a few attempts I gave up and, seeing the rather unusual type of family, I told the woman that she should come to the parish church for the other catecheses.

My life as a deputy parish priest was a continual battle. When priests explained the Catholic doctrine in their sermons and in the catecheses, they had to be careful, to avoid reactions that at times could be very heated. However, there were also very rewarding experiences. I recall moments spent with people suffering with incurable diseases, with whom I stayed up to the moment of death.

Many of these terminally ill people, including those that had lost their faith, made their confession, received the anointment of the sick and took Communion before dying.

You say, 'Priests had to be careful to avoid heated reactions at Mass'. What do you mean?

At that time the most sensitive points, those that created clashes, concerned morals and the liturgy. For example, the celebration of the First Communion with a eucharistic prayer selected from those already existing and approved (that is, not one made up there and then) and keeping to the Roman Missal for the other parts, often led to a tiresome battle with the parents responsible for the ceremony, and required great diplomacy. The same applied to the celebration of marriages, when the couple wanted at all costs non-Biblical readings and other things that were liturgically unacceptable, even going as far as asking for words that did not include the indissolubility of marriage.

Those who did not see their demands satisfied sometimes went to another priest, in a nearby parish, who was willing to accept anything. The problems that we had thirty years ago with marriages have today moved to funerals: these are the people of the same generation, who are now old, who insist on adapting the funeral liturgies to suit their wishes. These are circumstances experienced by every Dutch priest that is determined to proclaim the true Catholic faith.

But, apart from funerals, how are things going now?

Now, more than thirty years after my ordination as a priest, almost all the parishes have taken the preparation for the First Communion and the Confirmation away from the Catholic schools, so as to be free to decide on the content of the catechesis and also to avoid endless discussions on the liturgy. This is also done in order to prepare the children who are getting ready for the first Confession as well as for the first Communion, which had become another thorny issue in many schools. Furthermore, those who want to celebrate a sacramental marriage, even if they are few in number, are more open to the doctrine and also the liturgy of the Church. Perhaps they are not very knowledgeable, but do not display the hostility and the prejudices that were once evident.

When I was a young parish priest, there were still five Masses on Sundays: to be accurate, two celebrated on Saturday evenings, two on Sunday mornings and one in the evening. At 7 p.m. on Saturday and 11 a.m. on Sunday there was still a good number of worshippers. Now far fewer people come to church, but those that are still coming are stronger believers and lead a life of prayer, especially if they are young.

The wider context is far from simple. Recently there have been several sociological studies on faith, with results that are not exactly encouraging. According to one of these, carried out in 2016, entitled *God in Nederland*, 'God in Holland', in that year slightly more than half of Dutch Catholics believed that Jesus was the Son of God or, at least, was sent by God. Many Dutch people still know, more or less, what is celebrated at Christmas, that is, the birth of Jesus. But the significance of Easter and even more of Whitsun are more elusive.

We are all aware of stories of priests who have suffered under Communism for their faith and have courageously kept their beliefs. Amazing stories. Those priests, however, normally had one thing: a sizeable congregation who wanted to know Christ. This is the difference with the situation now in front of us: today in Western Europe the priest often meets resistance or, worse still, great indifference. If he defends the true Catholic faith, he is on trial and has to justify his views on moral issues. He must justify himself for the abuses committed in the Church by others.

One day in 2010, when the scandal of the sexual abuses of minors committed by priests and monks erupted also in Holland, the auxiliary bishop of Utrecht left the arch-bishop's residence on foot. A man passed him by on a bicycle and shouted out, 'Hey, paedophile, shouldn't you be in prison?' Many priests have had similar experiences.

How does a priest handle the strain and find the serenity, especially psychological serenity, to carry on?

A life like that is only bearable for a priest on three conditions.

His training as a priest must have been thorough and comprehensive, that is, at a human level, intellectual—with studies of philosophy and theology and with a background that allows him to talk to everybody in the parish—as well as spiritual. He must be a man who really prays, not just a man of devotions. In the seminary in the diocese of Roermond I had a traditional spiritual training with daily Mass, meditation, breviary and Rosary. A spiritual training in the Jesuit mould, which is a good foundation for a diocesan priest, but is not the only one. The church is well aware of the spirituality of the Car-melites, the Franciscans or the Benedictines and many others that are just as good for the life of a diocesan priest.

A second condition is that the priest should continue this lifestyle and this training after being ordained. In the parish this is difficult because of his many duties: the large number of sermons that a priest must prepare, the cate-cheses, the relations with his parishioners, the unexpected funerals and all the tasks related to management and administration. Life in the parish does not follow a routine as in the seminary. It is crucial for the seminarist to discover this during his pastoral apprenticeship and to be looked after by a mature priest that is able above all to make room for his training and his spiritual life within the hurly-burly of a parish. As I have already said, in this regard the priest of the parish where I grew up was a model for me even before I entered the seminary.

Much of this applies also to lay believers, who want to keep their faith in Christ in an environment that today is seriously secularised and even anti-Christian; but it applies above all to the life of a priest in his specific task of proclaiming the faith. In fact, the priest represents Jesus in person, first of all in celebrating the Eucharist, when the bread and the wine become the Body and the Blood of Christ, and in the administration of those sacraments where sins are pardoned, that is, those of the Reconciliation and of the Anointing of the sick.

I think that all of us do not believe enough in the importance of the sacraments.

Jesus wants to continue His life in us, as Saint John Eudes maintained. With baptism we are transfigured so as to resemble Jesus. This is reasserted in Confirmation, when the Holy Spirit gives us the strength to be Jesus' witnesses in this world. And the sacrament of the Eucharist nurtures our transfiguration in Jesus. Whereas ordinary nourishment is transformed into the substances of our body, in the case of the Eucharist the opposite happens: in receiving it, we are transformed into the Eucharist, that is, into Christ.

And in us Christ continues his life on earth, so that we, like Him, encounter the same difficulties that He Himself did, for example, in His many arguments with the scribes and the Pharisees. Martyrs mirror Him in their violent death, which they endure for their faith in Him. Jesus lives also his heavenly life in us, and this is revealed as well in a deep spiritual joy, an enormous strength for a human being.

Society, with all the technology that it can muster, can give us convenience and pleasure, but not spiritual joy. Only Christ can give it to us, because it is a gift from heaven. Whoever has savoured this spiritual joy once does not wish to lose it easily, and once it is savoured and lost, he will always feel something is missing in his life. This joy, the fruit of a close relationship with Jesus, does not satisfy the senses but the person in his totality, body and soul. It may be experienced only occasionally, but that does not matter: it is a deep strength that helps the believer remain a faithful follower of Christ.

Let's return to the three conditions you mentioned that make the life of a priest bearable. What is the third?

The third condition is that the priest has a regular contact with a spiritual guide, who may not necessarily be his confessor, but it is preferable if he is. This is advisable for a lay person as well. My experience as a bishop has taught me that a priest, but also a deacon or a lay person, who gets bogged down in pastoral activities as well as in his personal life, is often one who lacks a personal spiritual guide.

It is important to have the possibility of talking with a priest about your own inner life, of the difficulties and frustrations in the life outside and especially in your pastoral life. A good spiritual guide who has a deep relationship with Christ can recognise the mistakes, the errors of perspective and those elements of confusion that the person who consults him is not able to see in himself. And he can encourage him.

One day, when I said to my spiritual guide that bishops today spread the faith with great determination and fight to overcome so much resistance, and yet receive hardly any reward, he replied, 'This is the true life of bishops, of the successors of the apostles. Go and see in the *Acts of the Apostles* what their life and work were like'. Those words were and still are of great comfort to me. The priest needs to have the possibility of talking in secret of the burdens he feels in his soul, of his sins, of his temptations, of his inborn selfishness and its consequences. And he can do this in a productive way with a spiritual guide, who can help him to maintain pure and intact the training he had received in the seminary, to amend it and to widen it when necessary.

After defending my dissertation at the Angelicum, the Dominican university in Rome, I taught moral theology in the seminary where I had studied. These were wonderful years. The students were generally open to the teaching of ethics according to the doctrine of the Church. I gave many lectures, especially on the subject of bioethics, sometimes meeting approval, and sometimes not, depending on the relationship of the audience with the teaching of the Church. I also wrote a number of articles, some more scientific, others expressing my own views. From 1997 to 1999 I also taught for one semester each year at the Faculty of Theology in Lugano. I was appointed a permanent professor in February 1999 and was looking for an apartment, when, in the month of July, I realised that it was a rather impermanent permanence, as John Paul II had nominated me as Bishop of Groningen.

As a result, I went back to Holland to start an experience that was new and unexpected and was also a very difficult ordeal: it was at that point that I realised how much I needed a spiritual guide.

The first press conference after the news of my nomination and the first three weeks went well: in fact, better than expected, considering that the new bishop was a teacher of theology in a seminary that had the reputation of being 'conservative' appointed to a diocese that was well-known as 'progressive'. In the third week, however, the media had got hold of the texts that I was using for my lectures on moral theology. The fact that I was teaching that subject according to the instructions of the Church was seen as a very grave sin. In our society you are, in fact, free to have your own opinions, except when these opinions diverge from the dominant culture.

Eijk *contra gentiles*, one could say …

I must admit that I have also made some mistakes. Once, when I was dealing with a series of mediaeval documents in which the Popes forbade the baptism of Jews with the threat of violence, in my enthusiasm to defend the Church I wrote that the injustices towards the Jews that were blamed on Christians were exaggerated. In actual fact, over the centuries many Christians have committed acts of cruelty towards the Jews, this cannot be denied. I was sincerely sorry to have written such things and I said so in a meeting with a delegation of Jews. I have always had a good relationship with the Jewish world in Holland.

Anyway, I have taught moral theology in compliance with the promises I made during my ordination as a deacon, as a priest and then as a bishop, that is to proclaim faithfully the doctrine of the Church. I have been severely attacked, in Holland and also in Belgium, especially for my stance on the subject of homosexuality. More than once I found outside the bishop's residence in Groningen journalists accompanied by cameramen. And because the building had only one exit, I had no means of escape on those occasions. At that time I was also rather nervous about showing myself in public, walking in the street.

I was also accused of alleged hatred towards homosexuals by a priest in the diocese of Groningen, who had been suspended *a divinis* from 1974 because he had been elected to the Dutch Parliament and then to the European Parliament. A public prosecutor examined my writings and my speeches and then published his conclusions that proved my complete innocence.

I think it is easy to understand from this event as well when I say that the period in question was perhaps the most stressful in my life. Before my ordination as bishop I had to meet priests, deacons and lay people in the five deaconries of the diocese to explain my views. Almost everyone was hostile because of the picture of me that had been circulated. But many said to me later that when I was seen at close quarters I seemed a different person. As a bishop also I often happened to be told the same thing, a sign that meeting in person enables even deep-rooted prejudices to be overcome.

Fr George Laan, my old parish priest, often used to say that during the prayers for the offertory I should place myself spiritually on the paten, in order to integrate myself into the sacrifice of Christ. My episcopate in Groningen seemed to provide the opportunity to really live that aspect of the Cross.

However, the celebration when I was ordained bishop and took possession of the see of Groningen on 6 November 1999 was wonderful. In my finishing speech I even managed to get the congregation to laugh, by quoting the words of my optician in Amsterdam, who, one day when I went into his shop, greeted me with the words, 'Here's our walking press cutting', since he had often seen my name in the daily papers because of the controversies that I was sparking.

Outside the cathedral, there was a small group protesting against my nomination, who were kept at the appropriate distance away by the police. Among them there was also a Dominican, wearing his white habit. It was a small group, perhaps in part because of the weather: it was a cold day with a very strong wind and a lot of rain.

What effect did such a harsh experience have on you?

Certainly the tension that I lived through, caused both by the attacks that I endured and also the expectations that I felt had been placed on me, did not do any good to my health. I do not want to venture a cause-and-effect relationship, but it so happened that slightly more than a year after my ordination as bishop I was staying in a monastery in Germany, and while I was having breakfast, I was struck by a sudden paralysis of the left part of my body and also of one of my vocal cords. I had suffered the rupture of an artery in the brain, with a stroke in the brainstem.

A few weeks later I developed an intense pain on the left side of my face, also as a result of the damage to my brainstem. This pain was unbearable for almost two years. Later on it became less severe but it has never gone away completely. I spent three weeks in hospital and a further six weeks in a nursing home for my convalescence. A convalescence that lasted a long time, even after I returned home and followed an appropriate recovery programme.

In the hospital, which was Catholic, even though I had to stay in bed, I was able to join in the celebration of the Mass every day in the chapel. When I went to the nursing home, which was a lay institution, I was sad because I could not take part in the daily Mass. However, much to my surprise, the head nurse of the ward said to me, 'We know that you are a bishop and therefore we have bought a crucifix that you can put up on the wall'. I saw in this gesture a sign of the Lord, who was saying to me, 'You were asking yourself where I was, but I was already here, I got here before you'. Some days later my secretary brought me a small travelling case for celebrating the Mass, so that, sitting down, I was able to say Mass every day in my room.

For the first time in my life I found myself in a situation where I was unable to do anything but resign myself and be patient. I had always been very active, always involved in planning and organising something. I had a certain tendency to dwell on the exterior aspects of life, and this can easily lead to a corrosion of the interior life, a widespread problem in today's world. There is a risk of forgetting where the source is, the origin of everything: that is, in our interior life, where we can meet the One whom Saint Augustine called '*interior intimo meo*', who is nearer to us than we are to ourselves, that is, God.

It was precisely at that time that someone gave me the book by Cardinal Van Thuân, the then President of the Pontifical Council for Justice and Peace, entitled *The road of hope*. Van Thuân tells how he was made a prisoner by the Communist regime in 1975, two days after being appointed assistant bishop of Saigon; he was arrested by the police after the fall of South Vietnam. For nine years he was kept in a cell without windows. While he was suffocating from the heat and the humidity and feared losing his mind, he was tormented by the thought of his enforced neglect of his diocese and his work. One day, however, he heard a voice inside saying, 'Why are you tormenting yourself so much? You must draw a distinction between God and the works of God. All that you have done and that you want to continue doing … all this is splendid work. These are God's works, but they are not God! When God wishes you to give up all this work, do it immediately and have faith in Him! God can do those things infinitely better than you. He will entrust these works to others, more suitable. You have chosen God alone, not His works as well'.

This was a message for me too, and it could not have arrived at a better time. Attention to God must not be stifled by activism, however good it is: the forced interruption following my illness was an invitation to find again the correct balance between my interior life and my active life. However, I, too, had feelings of rebellion. Some people were already starting to speculate on my successor, something that was hurtful to me, even if there were times when I myself wondered whether I would ever return to the bishop's chair in Groningen. In the end it became clear that the Lord wanted me to continue as bishop of Groningen, but for a long time this was not obvious.

Anyway, I did not express my feelings to the people who came to visit me, but I found another safety valve: the *Liturgy of the Hours*.

The breviary? Why is it a safety valve?

The focal point of the *Liturgy of the Hours* is the *Psalms*. All the negative feelings that a human being can have are expressed in the *Psalms*. Faith in God is the central theme, although doubt and desperation are also to be found: 'My soul also is struck with terror, while you, O Lord—how long … I am weary with my moaning; every night I flood my bed with tears; I drench my couch with my weeping' (Ps 6:3, 6). 'Why, O Lord, do you stand far off? Why do you hide yourself in times of trouble?' (Ps 10:1). Those who read this, however much they are in darkness or are angry with God, keep in contact with Him.

We are in good company: Jesus also recited the *Psalms*. So the Church recites them together with the Lord; as Saint Augustine says: 'When we talk to God in prayer, we do not separate the Son from the Father, and when the

Body of the Son prays He does not separate His Head from Himself, but He Himself is the one and only saviour of His Body, our Lord Jesus Christ, who prays for us, prays in us and is prayed to by us. He prays for us as our priest, He prays in us as our Head and is prayed to by us as our God. Let us, therefore, recognise in Him our words and His words in us'.

Anyway, after ten months I was able to return to the diocese of Groningen, even if I was unsteady on my feet. It took nearly two years for my recovery, insofar as I was able to recover. Many thought that I would never be back, but it turned out differently. I started again. And seven years later Benedict XVI moved me to the archdiocese of Utrecht, where challenges different from those in Groningen awaited me; but that's another story.

What do you think of the 'Benedict option' as a Christian way of survival? I am referring to the bestseller by Rod Dreher, which has been much talked about.

If I consider what I see in the archdiocese of Utrecht, I think that this is a possible option, and there are early signs.

The fact that nowadays almost all the parishes no longer entrust the catechesis for the First Communion and the Confirmation to the schools, but want to do it themselves in order to ensure a good content, already points to a sort of withdrawal, in the Benedictine meaning of the word, on the part of the Church. There is, in fact, a way for the Church to withdraw from society that is good and must not be misunderstood. The Gospel must be proclaimed to everybody in this world. However, in order to evangelise the world again, the Church must also put its own house in order.

One of the intentions of the Second Vatican Council was for the Church to open up to society. The Church has done this, whereas society for its part has not opened up to the Church. On the contrary, it has driven it away from public life. Then the Church has fallen into one of the deepest crises of faith in its history and today it is not in the best position to pass on the faith to society. Many lay people and many pastors are confused about the contents of the faith. Only after having put its own house in order will the Church be really able again to evangelise the world.

In the High Middle Ages the Benedictine monasteries were the point of departure to achieve this. Today the monasteries still fascinate and attract. Those who take a spiritual retreat in a monastery, taking part in the daily Eucharist or in the *Liturgy of the Hours* with the community of monks, always achieve some benefits. And, thanks to the internet, when they cannot be physically present, they can still remain in contact with a monastic community, even at a distance, follow what they do, read the writings they produce and keep a spiritual connection alive.

But apart from monasteries, there are parishes that have continued to proclaim an authentic faith, that have held on to an authentic liturgy and have remained strong. In the second half of the 60s and in the 70s many priests tried to attract into church as many people as possible with experimental liturgies, even theatrical ones. Today in our archdiocese there are few priests, around fifty, and they all follow the Roman missal. Naturally they cannot celebrate Mass in all the 260 churches that we have—there is one parish priest who is responsible for fifteen churches—but I wanted the presence of one Eucharistic centre in every parish, in the most popular church, that is, where the Eucharist is always celebrated.

The experimental or creative liturgies have been, and, where they survive, still are, a great mistake, a path that leads to the achievement of nothing. Perhaps at the beginning these liturgies can be attractive to somebody, but in the end serious people look for a Mass that follows the authentic liturgy of the Church.

3

DICKENS'S DOCTOR

What did ecclesiastical celibacy cost you?

EVEN WHEN I was studying medicine I was thinking of the path to priesthood, and so I kept myself free from relationships. In the last two years, when I was doing my internship in hospital, and also during the year and a half when I was working as a doctor in one of the then hospitals of the University of Amsterdam, I met many female students and nurses. One nurse had fallen in love with me and she had made her feelings known. I made it clear to her that I was not interested, although I did not reveal my thoughts on the priesthood. She was disappointed, upset even, I think, but celibacy was the life I had chosen.

When I meet those preparing for confirmation in the archdiocese, and we talk of the Christian doctrine, of the sacrament they are about to receive, and of the Church, they ask me questions and often want to find out about this aspect of my life as a priest: 'Why are you forbidden from marrying?' 'But it is not the Church that forbids me to marry', I reply, 'I myself chose not to marry by becoming a priest, of my own free will', and I explain why a priest does not get married: because in that way his life is a reminder for the faithful of the existence of an eternal life in which there is no marriage and there are no matrimonial ties, as Jesus explains in the Gospels.

On one occasion a woman intervened saying that she did not agree. But one cannot disagree if one is not familiar with the faith, the Gospels, the Word of Jesus. The celibate life is of great significance for the Church and a great help for a priest.

Every state of life has difficulties to overcome. When I was deputy parish priest a married woman took a fancy to me and wrote me letters. I resolved the situation with the advice of my spiritual director and with the use of the right words and actions, because when people in love get rejected they can react very badly.

The celibate life is not in itself easy, but for me it has been a positive choice, an informed one, a case of 'I want to be celibate for Christ'. Celibacy makes you free and willing to dedicate yourself to the Church, a choice that is not available to someone who also has to look after a family. Saint Paul says as much in Corinthians:

> I want you to be free from anxieties. The unmarried man is anxious about the affairs of the Lord, how to please the Lord; but the married man is anxious about the affairs of the world, how to please his wife, and his interests are divided. (1 Cor 7:32–33).

But the ultimate principle for me is eternal life: celibacy, just as the vow of chastity for religious people, reflects the state that we will have when we rise again from the dead, it is a sign that reminds us how our life on earth is a taste of the true life that awaits us. In this sense the celibate life becomes in itself a proclamation of the Gospels. And just as in the sacrament of Marriage the husband and wife receive the grace to live their married life with the obligations that come with it, so in the sacrament of Ordination the priest receives the grace to live his state and his mission.

We must believe in the force of the sacraments. Married life also is not easy. When I take my walks, I sometimes go past a nursery school and see the parents collecting their children on their way back from work. A father and a mother who work all day, when they are at home they must dedicate themselves to the children, prepare dinner, get the housework done: it is a huge task and a huge responsibility. We must not exaggerate the difficulties of the celibate life.

What gives you most joy in your ministry?

I became a priest in order to celebrate the Eucharist. Many priests at the beginning have felt this desire, which is a sign of the priestly vocation. The daily celebration of the Mass has always been for me the summit of my day. 'Summit' is one of the terms used in the Second Vatican Council to describe the meaning of the Eucharist for the Christian life (see Vatican II, *Sacrosanctum Concilium* no. 10). This applies also to the Mass on weekdays, which is a simpler affair. It is not an emotional joy that it gives me, but a spiritual joy.

If I think of other joys, I remember some seminarians in the two dioceses where I have been whom I have subsequently ordained as priests. All of them are Dutch, except for one Colombian. The vocations we have are few, but they are good ones, also in terms of average age. And if I think to the future, to the next 50 years, this gives me hope and joy: to know that, although the number of priests will be limited, there will still be some. Priests are necessary to celebrate the Eucharist. And to give people the possibility of meeting Jesus in the Blessed Sacrament.

Naturally there are also moments that give less joy: in my case this was certainly the serious illness at the beginning of 2001 and the recovery that took ten months: a long time, that, however, taught me to say, like Saint Martin of Tours, '*noli recusare laborem*', I am still ready to do something in this life for You, Lord.

It is the motto that I chose when I became a bishop. But I understood its real meaning only in those months. When I had to resume work it was not easy, I still felt very tired.

Then in the course of two years the Lord allowed me to regain the strength that I had before.

That ordeal taught me to be patient. Before then I was very active but also impatient. I learnt to wait. To be a follower of Jesus requires patience, which also means the capacity to endure, as He did when he suffered on the cross. Therefore, I am also pleased with the rewards that that experience gave me. It is also wonderful for me to prepare sermons and catecheses, to spend time with young people, to talk to them of the beauty of the faith, to see their response, to see them approach Confession. But the greatest joy remains the celebration of the Eucharist.

'De Maria numquam satis', you can never say enough about Mary: this is the ancient motto repeated by many saints. Immediately after the Council, however, it seemed that, because of the many 'de Maria satis', enough had been said about her. Things have changed, but do you not think that in the Church that is now theologically more sophisticated there is a strange lukewarm attitude towards the the Mother of God?

Many theologians no longer pay much attention to the figure of Mary. There are many reasons, and there is also a problem of faith. If you do not believe in the incarnation of the Divine Word, of the Son of God, then the figure of Mary loses its significance. She becomes the mother of a man, a special man perhaps, but still a man.

The dogmatic constitution of the Council, *Lumen gentium* (no. 63) declares of Mary that she is the image of the Church and says that we should all be like her; but for some theologians she seems more like a devotion that belongs to the past.

However, with the people she is still relevant. And for many Mary is the single thread that keeps them still in contact with the Church: in their need they pray to her. Perhaps she is the one thing that they still hold on to from their family's Catholic roots. But Mary leads us to Jesus, and so, even if she is the only thread remaining, this thread is nevertheless very important.

When Mary has appeared, she has always done so to lead us to the Son, not to herself. In Utrecht I would say that devotion to Mary is still alive. Every three years the diocese organises a pilgrimage to Lourdes, with between 1,300 and 1,500 participants. Not all of them are really firm believers and practising Catholics, and there are always some who wonder why there needs to be a Mass every day and would like a lighter schedule. What strikes me, however, is that during the pilgrimage these people change their views and in the end they are always happy with the schedule, including the Eucharistic celebrations. It also strikes me seeing how many resume their religious practice and, when they are back in Holland, they return to the sacraments.

Through Mary they discover the richness of the liturgy, the splendour of the Eucharist, and many discover Confession. The importance of Mary's role in our salvation cannot be played down. On the road of life, when we lose our way, it is the signposts that help us find again the road to Christ.

Who are the converts in Holland today?

There are about 500 people converting to Catholicism in Holland every year. In most cases these are truly personal decisions, informed and serious. They discover the Church. Some have been baptised but are Protestants, though the majority have not been baptised. Starting from as early as the beginning of the last century and gradually growing in numbers, there is now a wide band of the population that has never been baptised and has never heard anything of the Gospels, or of Christ, except for a few notions learnt in their youth or some negative comments that have appeared in the media.

Once in Groningen Cathedral I baptised a man of around fifty and also administered Confirmation and his first Holy Communion. On his way to work this person used to pass by the cathedral every day. He told me that he felt mysteriously drawn to that church. One day he went in and, all alone, in the silence of the church, he simply decided to become a Catholic. What he saw in the cathedral, which could have left another person completely indifferent, was for him a real encounter with Christ. It was certainly the Holy Spirit that had inspired that visit, that step. And the first time he entered the church he converted. There was nobody acting as an intermediary, there were no external causes. That man came to Christ inspired by the Holy Spirit. He was a sincere person, that was immediately clear.

Here in Utrecht Cathedral I give the sacrament of Confirmation to those who have not been able to receive it in their parish because of illness or for other problems. I meet people who want to receive Confirmation so that they can get married, including non-practising Catholics; but there are also true conversions, of Dutch people who discover the Church and, through the Church, Christ. Normally they know people within their community who are believers, and they become curious, talk to these people and ask questions. They come into contact with the fire of the faith, which by its very nature spreads out and envelops whatever it meets. True believers have a special influence on the social environment where they live, even before they talk of their faith.

The church of Saint Willibrord in Utrecht is of ancient and moving beauty. How come the diocese sold it?

Cardinal Bernard Alfrink, famous for the role he played in the Council and who was Archbishop of Utrecht from 1955 to 1975, deconsecrated this church at the end of the 60s. These were the years we mentioned, when attendance at Mass collapsed. Funds were needed to restore the church, but they were starting to become scarce. In addition, the cathedral and the church of Saint Augustine were actually close by.

So Alfrink took the decision to close Saint Willibrord and to sell the parish to which the church belonged to a developer who had plans to pull everything down and then build luxury apartments, given that the area was, and still is, very central. He would make a lot of money. However, at a certain point this developer must have had an experience similar to yours, that is, he realised that the church was a real gem. And remember that the neogothic style of Saint Willibrord was no longer popular at that time. In short, the developer did not have the heart to demolish the church, and so he sold it to a foundation that organised cultural events for gain, even if another Catholic foundation with a pastoral purpose also became involved in the management of the church.

The economic problems recurred, because the church still needed work to be carried out, but the foundation that owned it could not afford it. In the end the city of Utrecht paid, except for 1.7 million euro, a debt that needed to be repaid, but nobody knew by whom. But other problems also came to light: the foundation that owned the building included anti-Catholic people, who organised blasphemous events, such as a play that was a parody of the Mass. The church was desecrated. It was no longer a sacred place, suitable for divine worship. The foundation refused to reach an agreement with us as to what activities to hold there in the future.

It was at that moment that the Society of Saint Pius X came on to the scene: they made an offer that was accepted, and so bought the church and settled the debt. Subsequently I invited the rector of the church and the head of the Society for the Benelux countries. We had a pleasant meeting and established a good relationship. We must not have too high expectations as regards the timescale, but I think that at a certain point the complete and manifest union with the Society of Saint Pius X will be reached once more.

What do you think of the *Motu proprio Summorum Pontificum* of Benedict XVI? Since then the liturgy in the *vetus ordo*, in the ancient rite, has started to spread again, even if there is still some resistance.

I was an altar-boy with the *vetus ordo*. I have to say that that liturgical reform, for us lads, the assistants, did not seem at all necessary, that's what I remember. On the other hand, we were of an age when we did not understand everything, so we simply followed the instructions that we were given. However, I remember that for the old parish priest the change was very difficult: he had been ordained perhaps during the First World War and had been celebrating the Tridentine rite for almost 50 years.

I myself am not capable of celebrating in the *vetus ordo*, it is complex and needs to be done with care. On one occasion I was indeed invited to celebrate the ordination of a deacon in the *vetus ordo*, but I had to decline the invitation as I cannot do it. Nowadays my time is limited, so for me to learn another rite is demanding. But I have some priests in the diocese that are capable of celebrating in the *vetus ordo*.

Some people had asked me to have a Mass with the ancient rite on a regular basis in the diocese, so that they would not have to go to Amsterdam every time, where the Priestly Fraternity of Saint Peter have their own church and where they celebrate the Mass in accordance with the Tridentine rite. I sent them to one of the priests in my archdiocese who is able to celebrate in the *vetus ordo*, but he replied, 'Your Eminence, I am ready to do it right now, but I don't have the time ... ' To be fair, he happens to be a parish priest who has the largest parish in the diocese, with 35,000 Catholics.

It should be borne in mind too that the readings in the two rites are different, so that a priest would also have to prepare two different Sunday sermons. The commitment required is very demanding compared to the number of priests that we have. However, there is another priest here in Utrecht, in the church of Saint Raphael, who celebrates the Mass in the *vetus ordo* in the cathedral once a month.

Modern Holland has been a Protestant country, it is a Protestant monarchy, and also in its colonial history it spread Protestantism. Was it not difficult for a Dutch Catholic to feel he is part of such a national history?

Holland was a Protestant nation, it's true. On this point I should like to make it clear that the Protestants had already lost their majority back in the 30s of the last century, as a result of the major reduction in the size of the families, partly due to the spread of contraception in the last years of the nineteenth century. And then many started to leave the national Reformed Church, as we have already mentioned.

Having said that, don't forget that in Holland the Catholics have worked more abroad as missionaries, compared to the Protestants. The Lutherans, for example, did very little missionary work, the Calvinists more. Even before the restoration of the Catholic hierarchy in the country, there was the presence of religious congregations, who were very active in the colonies, from Indonesia to Suriname. After the restoration of the Catholic hierarchy Dutch Catholicism developed very rapidly: we built many churches, there was a flood of people taking holy orders, including as missionaries. It has been calculated that in 1960 about 11% or 12% of all the missionaries active in the world came from our country.

So there was more Catholicism in the soul of the country than it seemed.

Yes, although problems of coexistence between us and the Protestants still existed and lasted a long time. The return of the Catholic hierarchy did not resolve these difficulties. Here in Utrecht there was a strong presence of Calvinists, who are very inflexible.

The bishops were not seen in a good light and tried to keep a low profile. The first Archbishop of Utrecht after the restoration of the hierarchy in 1853, Joannes Zwijsen, was also bishop of 's-Hertogenbosch and lived there. Another three archbishops who succeeded him lived in the clergy house of the cathedral so as not to attract too much attention. In 1898 Archbishop Hendrik van de Wetering bought the property where I live today, and also built the beautiful neo-Gothic chapel that we have restored as part of the reconstruction works of the arch-bishop's residence. But he did not buy the building directly, which would have involved many problems, but through an intermediary. In fact, the owners would have never sold the property to a Catholic bishop.

This was the state of affairs that still existed at the end of the nineteenth century and the beginning of the twentieth.

In your opinion, why do the supporters of a 'liberal' theology and of a 'liberal' Church (as they say in the Anglo-Saxon world) seem unaware of the sterility to which that model of Christianity leads?

The aim of 'liberal' theology is to make the faith palatable to the modern and, as you might say, enlightened man. This was also the intention of liberal Protestant theologians in the nineteenth century. Half a century later, this approach has caused an appalling haemorrhage of churchgoers. In this country we say that liberal theology is killing itself, because it does not convey the true faith, the true Christ.

When we proclaim the true faith, the Holy Spirit causes it to swell in the hearts of the faithful. We must proclaim and convey the content of the faith, but the faith itself is given by the Holy Spirit. And the Spirit does not operate along the path of liberal theology, but along the path of the authentic faith of the Church. When the essential elements of the message of Jesus are changed, the Spirit does not reveal Himself. This causes the sterility that you have mentioned. We must always start from the deposit of faith (*Depositum fidei*) and maintain it.

There is often talk of Christians being persecuted in certain 'hot' areas of the world. But those who truly want to be Christians are already persecuted in tolerant secular Europe, as can be deduced from what you have said.

Christianity is the most persecuted religion in the world: so many lose their life every year for being faithful to Christ! We must pray for them, support them and encourage them.

When the Pope creates a new cardinal he says a very important thing: that he must be ready to shed his blood for his faith in Christ, and the red colour of his habit is a reference to martyrdom. Life is an intrinsic good, but faith in Christ is a higher good. Sometimes we hear martyrs referred to as suicides: they are not suicides, they are Christians who are killed by others for their devotion to Christ.

Having said this, we certainly must not forget that in our countries as well, in Western Europe, Christians are persecuted. Nowadays it is more and more difficult to live and work whilst remaining faithful to Catholic ethics, it can entail serious difficulties and many sacrifices.

I know a woman doctor who has also worked as a volunteer in our cathedral, and she is frequently asked to perform euthanasia. She has never done it and the patients have turned to other doctors, but she is constantly put under pressure, she has to battle all the time in order not to betray her own principles. This woman will not lose her life, but she does not have and will never have an easy professional life. The pain can be very great.

The Dutch law on abortion states that no medical practitioner can be compelled to carry it out. The clause relating to conscientious objection was demanded by the Christian members of Parliament. Conscientious objection is also accepted in the case of euthanasia, although it was not inserted in the text of the law. However, the employer, the management committee of a hospital that offers euthanasia, can appoint other doctors or dismiss those who do not want to abide by certain protocols.

At the beginning of the 80s there was a famous case: three Calvinist nurses refused to be involved in abortions: one was dismissed and another was moved to a different department. They sued, but the judge backed the hospital.

The Church is defying the world also as regards its view of homosexuality; you have spoken of the attacks you endured in Groningen on this subject.

Yes, it is a much-disputed issue and many people have problems with the Catholic point of view. The Church is perhaps the only 'organisation' on a global scale today that considers the homosexual act as intrinsically evil, according to Revelation, Tradition and the documents of the magisterium, which are very clear.

Unfortunately today many pastors appear to be divided and confused, and increase the confusion among the faithful: I'm thinking also of the so-called 'theory of gender'. In 2019 I gave a talk on the subject of gender at the annual international pro-life forum held in Rome. This was at the Pontifical University of Saint Thomas Aquinas.

After the text of my speech was published, I received messages from many parts of the world, from people who thanked me for speaking out clearly. I did not receive any negative reactions. However, a Dutch journalist ridiculed me in his blog regarding an interview on gender that I had given after the conference.

I see many believers who in this climate of confusion feel themselves abandoned and isolated, and some of them are starting to have doubts about established teachings. This is certainly not the first time in the history of the Church that elements of the doctrine are challenged. At some point the Holy Spirit, who guides the Church on the path to Truth, will lead us to overcome this crisis. But it could take a long time.

For many people another source of worry is the work of the Synod that has been set up in Germany, which is focused on issues such as the celibacy of priests, the role of women in the Church, the power within the Church and sexual morality. The German Conference of Bishops,

incidentally, has not stated that there is a direct link
between the sexual morality of the Church and the sexual
abuses in the Church, but has made a number of proposals
and has indicated that in any case there is a need to look
again at Catholic ethics on sexuality in order to confront
the subject of the abuses. Let's hope that we can avoid the
umpteenth source of confusion for the faithful.

**Speaking of Germany, after Luther broke away, the
next pope was a Dutchman: Adrian VI, who was, like
yourself, Archbishop of Utrecht.**

Yes, he was born here in the city, we know the location of
the house where he was born. His father was a carpenter,
his family was of modest origins, but he had a splendid
career: he became professor of moral theology at the
University of Louvain, tutor of Charles V and was his
representative in Spain. He saved Spain for Charles V. And
he was elected pope without attending the conclave, a very
unusual event. He learnt of his election only a couple of
weeks later.

**The seminaries: there are those would like to change
them, those who would like to abolish them and those
who defend the current set-up. What do you think?**

I think that the seminary is still something that the Church
needs. In 2009 I had unfortunately to close down our own
for lack of funds, and consequently send my seminarians
to the one in the diocese of Haarlem. Later on their
number increased to such an extent that I decided to
reopen the seminary, but in a more modest form, with
reduced costs.

The students attend the Faculty of Theology in Utrecht,
of which I am the Chancellor and which was recognised
by Rome on 1 January 2007. It was born out of the

amalgamation of two theological faculties, that of Tilberg and that of Utrecht itself. Formally this is a faculty of Tilberg University, but its premises are here in Utrecht.

In Holland we have two Catholic Universities, that of Nijmegen, perhaps the better known abroad, and that of Tilberg. But the Faculty of Theology, obviously, does not undertake the training of priests or their spiritual development, this is not its task: it is up to the archdiocese to do that. Also the seminarians from the dioceses of Breda and Rotterdam come to the Theological Faculty in Utrecht. And the seminarians from the diocese of Groningen live in our seminary. Rotterdam has its own seminary, but, as regards their spiritual development, the seminarians come to us.

When you go to the Vatican, what is your impression of the Roman Curia?

I had a number of difficult issues to deal with as Bishop of Groningen, and as Archbishop of Utrecht I had to reorganise many things in the archdiocese to avoid bankruptcy, and consequently I have often consulted the Congregation for the Clergy, the Congregation for Catholic Education for the Faculty of Theology, and other departments.

I must say that they have always helped me in a friendly way and with great professionalism. I have also always been welcomed in their offices. Consequently I can say that I have received real help from the staff of these two congregations, also in guiding me through the twists and turns of canon law so as to avoid mistakes.

At all times it is necessary to act with caution and precision, as errors, especially regarding formal aspects, are always just round the corner, with damaging consequences.

As for the cases of sexual abuse that have taken place in the diocese I have also consulted the Congregation for the Doctrine of the Faith where I have also received important and expert help. And so the impression I have had of the Roman Curia has been good, absolutely good. It is often spoken of in a negative way, but that is not my experience. Which does not mean that there are no problems. All I am saying is that I happened to find dedicated people, who displayed Christian compassion and a spirit of service to the Church that I considered authentic. On more than one occasion I was impressed by this. My experience over the years with the papal nuncios in Holland has also been positive.

What are your memories of the 2013 conclave?

I never imagined that I would take part in a conclave a year after being made a cardinal. I heard the news of the resignation of Benedict XVI like many others, when Roland, my secretary, phoned me to ask if I knew anything about the rumours that were going around. I said that I hadn't and that, on the contrary, it seemed to me to be a joke in very poor taste. After a few minutes everything became clear.

I remember Benedict XVI's farewell speech on 28 February 2013, his meeting with the College of Cardinals, he seemed very nervous. I have never seen him since that day. Then there was the famous journey by helicopter towards Castel Gandolfo.

After that I remained in Rome. There were many cardinals like me that had had no experience of a conclave and didn't know exactly what to do, until Cardinal Sodano sent us a letter with information and instructions. There were 13 general congregations before the election of the Pope, while we were waiting for the arrival of the last cardinal, the archbishop of Saigon. When he arrived, he was greeted with great applause, and we could finally set a date for the beginning of the conclave, Tuesday 12 March.

After five ballots Cardinal Bergoglio was elected Pope. It was an emotional event. I had never had the chance to look at the frescos of Michelangelo so intently as in those days. In the pauses between one ballot and another, other cardinals also would get up to admire the scenes of the Last Judgement. They inspired meditation. Before putting the ballot sheet in the box on the altar of the Chapel, we were required to make a very powerful statement, one that goes right to the heart. Other cardinals, too, told me that they felt the same sensation. Because I had to repeat the words five times, they have remained in my memory: 'I call as my witness Christ the Lord, who will be my judge, that my vote is given to the one who before God I think should be elected'.

I stayed in Rome for more than three weeks, obviously cancelling all the engagements that I had in my diary, and this was perhaps the longest period that I spent without interruption in the Holy City. A period of intensive work. During the general congregations, before the conclave, there was the chance to make a speech, and not just for a few minutes as in the Synod, but for as long as necessary. Many took advantage of this chance, and I also spoke about issues that I considered urgent, some on the subjects of bioethics. These were important moments, also because the majority of the cardinals did not know one another before this. Taking meals together gave us another opportunity to get a better idea of certain cardinals.

I want to draw your attention to this passage from the text written by Benedict XVI on the problem of sexual abuses in the Church, which was very controversial when it became public in 2019: 'There are values that it is never right to sacrifice in the name of a still higher value, and which are even higher than the preservation of the physical life. God is more important even than physical survival. A life that is 'bought' at the price of denying God, a life based on an extreme lie, is a non-life. Martyrdom is a fundamental category of the Christian existence. The idea that martyrdom is basically no longer morally necessary, as in the theory advocated by [Franz] Böckle and many others, puts at stake the very essence of Christianity'. It raises a fundamental issue: on the one hand, we are losing the category of martyrdom in Christian life, according to Ratzinger, that is, the belief that there are acts that must never be carried out, even at the cost of life if necessary, while, on the other hand, we are faced by new arguments centred on 'the greatest possible good'. What do you think?

Absolute rules, that is, rules that do not allow any exceptions, are no longer acceptable in our society. Instead, a theory of situational ethics has taken hold, a theory that was first put forward by liberal Protestants. Furthermore, since the 60s, Catholic moral theology has entered into crisis, with the spread of the theory of the fundamental option and of *proportionalism* or *consequentialism*. For instance, these theories have led to the idea that abortion is indeed a physical evil, but, in order to decide whether it is also a moral evil, it must be viewed in the light of the purpose for which it is carried out. On this basis, even contraception can have a good purpose.

According to *proportionalism*, when the good of the goal and the physical evil of the means of achieving that goal are placed face-to-face, leading to the conclusion that there is a proportionate reason between the two, then it follows that abortion or the use of contraceptives is morally good. The fundamental point is that the existence of absolute truth is denied, and, instead, public opinion is ruled by complete relativism. However, relativism contradicts itself by positing as the unalterable truth that there is no unalterable truth.

Because it rejects any other views, relativism becomes dictatorial. When someone criticises this relativism, he is accused of being a fundamentalist and becomes marginalised. They advocate autonomy, personal liberty, but forget the existence of a real dictatorship, that of public opinion.

A Belgian author wrote a criticism of the theory of gender from the Catholic perspective. A scientist reacted saying in essence that this was the product of a schizophrenic mind. In other words, he called him mad. He did not criticise the argument the writer had put forward—that it is not possible to completely separate gender, that is, the social role of man and woman, from biological sex—but unequivocally dismissed the writer as unworthy even of being considered.

Those who defend Catholic doctrine are treated as crazy. In the Western world this stance is more and more widespread and many Catholics are intimidated, they cannot find the courage to proclaim the doctrine of the Church, their own beliefs. Even among priests and bishops you see this reluctance to speak out. They are severely attacked when they put forward the Catholic doctrine, especially in the area of morals, concerning marriage and sexual ethics.

I myself faced this situation after I was appointed Bishop of Groningen. Some of my words were taken out of context, in order to create the image of a monster: it was an attack that lasted four months and was repeated later. Nevertheless, we must speak openly of the doctrine of the Church.

From many parts of the world I receive positive reactions from the faithful who feel encouraged when bishops and cardinals have the strength to say the truth. We must have the courage to speak out without restraint, without fear, as John Paul II urged us to do many times. We have the great responsibility to tell people the truth, and must carry on the work of Jesus, through the sacraments, but also by proclaiming His divine word. And people have the right to know it. It does not matter how strong the opposition is, we must have the courage to say that Jesus is our saviour and that salvation is found only in Him. Our duty is to do everything possible to ensure that people do not end up in Hell.

I once met a priest who said to me, 'I think of what Jesus has commanded us to do, and I wonder if we are doing enough to proclaim the Christian faith'. He was saying this in all seriousness, it was a question that disturbed him profoundly. And it is a question that we should all ask ourselves.

Why do we speak so little of eternal life? It sometimes seems like an appendage to the sermon. But it should be at the heart of it.

Yes, it is something we speak of very little. Sometimes we feel a sort of embarrassment, sometimes even an anxiety about how some people will react. On one occasion in a sermon I spoke of the devil, something, incidentally, that also Pope Francis often does, and a woman complained because she did not consider it appropriate: in her opinion, it was a subject to be avoided, we must not frighten people. But the devil is a real person, who tries to seduce us, and we must put people on their guard against his presence. When I was a deputy parish priest, 35 years ago, the churches were still relatively crowded, but many no longer believed in the Last Things. Now there are far fewer believers, but those that remain believe these truths much more firmly, and so reactions are different from in the past.

In our sermons, in our catecheses we must talk of Paradise, of our glorious destiny, of the joyful vision that awaits us as saved souls. To see God face to face. On the other side there is Purgatory and also Hell, where we are separated from God, and this is a source of endless suffering. We must talk of these things, because without the resurrection and the eternal life Christian life loses its meaning. Then Jesus is simply a great teacher and Christianity is just a philosophy with strong ethical connotations, just as stoicism was.

I was asked to make a podcast, on Hell, Purgatory and Paradise, on the Internet site of the Dutch Episcopal Conference. To do this I used a poem by Saint John Henry, Cardinal Newman, *The Dream of Gerontius*. The protagonist is Gerontius, a person who did not lead a good life. Before his death he asks his friends to pray for him and then receives the last rites from a priest and dies. After his death Gerontius cannot see anything anymore, he is disorientated because his soul is separated from his body, and so he no longer has his senses available to him. His guardian angel, who had watched over him in life, leads him to Jesus, where he is allowed for a moment to see the eyes of the Lord full of love. At that moment Gerontius realises that he is not able to bear the gaze of Jesus for all eternity and he himself asks to be able to go through a purification. The Lord agrees and the angel takes him to Purgatory.

The meaning of Purgatory is, therefore, the realisation that we have not yet reached the goal for which we have been created, the joyful vision of God for eternity. There are also those who, faced with the eyes of Jesus, reject that gaze, for ever. This is their choice, which is respected by God, and these people are separated from Him for all eternity. Their whole life led to this choice. We can understand this if we think of what happens on earth: a virtuous person instinctively looks for the company of virtuous people, an evil person is drawn to people similar to him. This also applies to our relationship with God: once we have acquired the human virtues through our own efforts and have received the theological virtues and the gift of the Holy Spirit as a grace, and then have been redeemed by Jesus, at that point we shall be ready to look into his eyes full of love.

The flames of Hell and the fire of Purgatory are an image of the suffering derived from not being able to achieve, for ever or just to start with, the goal for which we were created. When a boy falls in love with a girl and she rejects him, the boy experiences a burning pain, like a fire in the heart.

Once I used *The Dream of Gerontius* also in a catechesis with some youngsters, and saw in them an opening up of their minds, a serene understanding of the ultimate realities. A reaction similar to that which accompanied the publication of Newman's poem in England. Some exponents of the Protestant world were also struck by his 'dream' and his vision of Purgatory.

Do you think about death?

During my preparation for the First Communion they talked about death, about eternal life, and this made a very strong impression on me. Since then the thought of death has been with me all the time. Death is for me a release from a difficult life, as a Christian, as a priest, as a bishop. However, I, too, must ask myself if I am ready to see the eyes of Jesus full of love.

My predecessor used to say that he hoped to end up at least in Purgatory. The possibility that God can grant us a period of purification is, I think, a very comforting message that helps to face death. Death that is a pain: Saint Thomas defines the separation of the soul from the body as the most terrible thing that can happen in our life. But we know that through the death on the Cross of Jesus, with which he has redeemed us, we are able to reach Paradise, even if we have to go through Purgatory. This gives great strength.

Is there a place where you like to retreat in prayer?

For my spiritual retreats I choose monasteries: last year it was a monastery of Capuchin nuns and this year of Benedictines in Italy. I like to stay in a community that prays, a contemplative community that also recites the *Liturgy of the Hours*, in which I can take part, and where I can meditate on the Scriptures.

For these moments of retreat a spiritual guide had advised me to read the Holy Bible first-hand and not other books, in which, however good they may be, there is always a person placing himself between us and God.

The organ teacher that I have mentioned, who lived in my village, was Protestant. A true Protestant: after meals he always read the Bible, every day. He read the Bible with passion, and the members of his family would listen attentively. I have learnt from that teacher something about the central position that the Word of God must have in our lives, something that I had not experienced in my family and a sensitivity that was not yet present among Catholics in the 70s. More so today. One of the benefits of the liturgy introduced by Paul VI is that, through the daily readings during the Mass and through the breviary, in three years one can cover almost the whole Bible.

Today the Church seems very divided. It seems that there are at least two Churches that are basically irreconcilable. How do we solve this problem?

Many people talk of the danger of a schism, but I do not think so. Rather I think that what has already happened with us in Holland will occur in many parts of the world. A silent process of healing has taken place because of the generational change. The priests of 1968, who had been ordained in those years of confusion, with ultra-progressive ideas, have almost disappeared or at least are no longer parish priests. Only a few of them, quite old, still have the energy to carry out some apostolates, but they are dealing with a different generation. If I think of the many young seminarians that I know in Italy, I have the impression that there will be a healing in Italy as well.

But it may take a long time, at least a generation. However, it will affect both clergy and lay people. Because, in the end, who will remain in the Church? In Holland those left are those that believe, that pray, that have a personal relationship with Christ. With the new generations of believers you can talk of Paradise or Hell without causing uproar, you can speak of the true content of our faith without people objecting or leaving the room to make their point, as was happening in the past.

I repeat, it takes time; we must have a great deal of patience and great trust in the strength of the Holy Spirit.

And while this process of renewal is taking place, we must be courageous and be prepared to suffer. When a person is a true believer, he suffers when he sees the crisis of faith that there is in the Church, the betrayals, the scandals. The true believer suffers, but remains faithful. And those that will remain in the Church will be the true believers. I am confident of this.

I am reminded of a cardinal that suffered and to the end remained faithful to the Church and to truth: Carlo Caffarra. What memory do you have of him?

I remember him as a great man. In the year 1987–1988 I was able to attend his course on the general ethics of sexuality at the Pontifical John Paul II Institute. Every so often I recall his image, quite a short man, sitting with a concentrated gaze, his elbows on the desk, while he ran his hand through his hair.

He had the reputation to be strict, whereas he was a calm and gentle person, who was always very open to his students. He was very fond of us, it was clear, and we also were fond of him. He was a son of scholastic theology, with a way of arguing that was very rigorous, methodical, precise, made up of premises and consequences. In this respect he was a true Thomist.

The writings of John Paul II on sexuality are very beautiful, but are not always equally easy to understand, they do not have that crispness that we find in the writings of Caffarra. On one occasion somebody pointed out to me that when Cardinal Caffarra gave lectures on subjects such as *Humanae vitae* or on sexuality, he always generated heated reactions, whereas when other lecturers spoke on the same subjects, everything proceeded very smoothly. I think that this actually was due to Caffarra's argumentative powers, which could be annoying to those who were not willing to accept the logical consequences of certain premises. It was as if Caffarra prevented his interlocutors from running away when they were unwilling to admit to being wrong.

Like John Paul II, also Caffarra developed an anthropological analysis of marriage and sexuality, which was needed in the Church after *Humanae vitae*. Paul VI had reaffirmed a fundamental moral truth, that is, that contraception is an intrinsic evil. John Paul II and Cardinal Caffarra worked very hard to explain this truth. The theology of the body that John Paul II developed is still wonderful and very important, but, I fear, not so easy to understand by the majority of the faithful. Caffarra was easier to follow.

I feel I should add that in the last part of his life he appeared more daring than many of his colleagues, even if they shared his opinions.

Because he carried Christ's truth in his heart. Caffarra was both rather timid and, at the same time, very brave. He used to defend his point of view very firmly.

I remember a conference at the Pontifical Lateran University where Caffarra had been invited to speak on *Humanae vitae*. Following on from what I said just now, I remember the tension that could be felt in the room among certain teachers and students at the Lateran University. There was no similar tension among students and staff at the John Paul II Institute.

A Dutch student who prepared his university dissertation with Caffarra went to see him after that academic event, and told me that he had found him a bit saddened by the reception he had received, but still very relaxed. He never gave any ground on moral truth, even when the media attacked him and tried to ridicule him. He never gave way one jot. He was a person who would have been willing to die for Christ, to be a martyr. This is the message he used to give.

Where do you see the presence of Satan today?

I want to start by reminding you that there are many devils, and then I should say that in the last two centuries Satan has done everything possible to make us think he does not exist. Many no longer see his influence.

Earlier we were talking of the suffering of a believer because of the situation of the Church today, all the scandals, the doctrinal problems, the shrinking of the Christian fabric. The devil operates by feeding a sense of scepticism, of profound sadness in the soul of the believer. He wants to see less enthusiasm in following Jesus, he wants there to be less charity and hope. We always need to be on guard, the devil is very cunning and works in a very insidious way.

Do you not think that it would be a step forward for everybody, but especially for the current hierarchy, to speak less, to write fewer papers that nobody reads, and pray more?

There was a period when in the Dutch Church as well we held many meetings, with big discussions … The most important thing is to participate in the celebrations of the Eucharist, when we receive and meet Christ in person. It is the most precious gift that we have in this world. Then Eucharistic adoration, silent prayer in the presence of Christ.

On the first Sunday in Advent in the month of December 2019 we started a Eucharistic year in our archdiocese. I produced a catechistic letter because many people do not know anymore what the Eucharist is. I explained what the Eucharist is about, what we celebrate, and I gave some practical guidance. And indeed I spoke of the adoration of the Most Holy Sacrament.

I see that various parish priests would like to set aside some hours for Eucharistic adoration, and there are a number that already do so. The days dedicated to the pastoral care of the young in the archdiocese of Utrecht end with an hour of Eucharistic adoration when there is the possibility of going to confession. Some years ago I organised a conference on Confession among other things and almost all the young people present went to confession.

Experience tells me that nowadays the young are very appreciative of silent prayer, of Eucharistic adoration, and do not have prejudices against the sacrament of Confession if it is explained and celebrated appropriately. Thirty years ago all this would have seemed impossible in Holland. This too teaches us that the situation can change.

In 2018, the German Episcopal Conference voted by a large majority in favour of directives that implied the possibility for a Protestant man married to a Catholic woman to receive the Eucharist, in so-called intercommunion. On that occasion you wrote a comment that ended in this way: 'I cannot avoid thinking of article 675 of the *Catechism of the Catholic Church* that says, "Before Christ's second coming the Church must pass through a final trial that will shake the faith of many believers. The persecution that accompanies her pilgrimage on earth will unveil the mystery of iniquity in the form of a religious deception offering men an apparent solution to their problems at the price of apostasy from the truth"'. Do you still think the same?

Naturally we do not know when this world will end. Jesus says in the Gospels that not even the angels nor the Son Himself know, only the Father. It's obvious that we must be very cautious: so many disasters and periods of crisis have been interpreted by contemporaries as signs of the end of time.

I wrote what you have quoted to put people on their guard, when they hear talk of Communion given to non-Catholics, outside the limits set by the *Code of Canon Law*, and talk of cardinals defending the blessing of homosexual couples, as a rite of pseudo-marriage. I thought of what we read in the *Catechism*, of the fact there will be a great apostasy before the end of the world and that an 'easy solution' will be offered to men for their problems, a deception.

The trends in moral theology denying the existence of absolute rules offer people easy solutions to the challenges they face. What the *Catechism* describes makes us think of our time, also of the behaviour of those who have been called to proclaim the truth in the Church. At the end of time the Antichrist will show himself in his greatest power, but we know that he is already active in the present. In the Gospels Jesus put us on our guard on various occasions. Our task is to proclaim the faith and live the faith. We know, in fact, that the end of this world means the return of Christ.

We started by talking of ordinary things. I should like to end in the same way: what do you read in your free time?

I like nineteenth-century literature, I like various Dutch writers of that period for whom Christianity was still an essential element of the society they described. Then the Russian classics, again of the nineteenth century, especially Dostoevsky, but also Tolstoy. And also English literature of the same period.

Recently I listened to an audiobook of *Bleak House* by Dickens, a rather complex novel and very good. Among the many characters there is a boy, homeless, called Jo. He is very good, the emblem of absolute poverty, of the miserable life to which many similar characters in Victorian England were subjected. Nobody cares about him and many are repelled by his scruffy appearance. Eventually an ex-soldier takes him home, but he falls ill with smallpox and then dies. The person who tries to treat him is Allan Woodcourt, a doctor who is a believer, who, when Jo is at the end of his life, tries to get him to say the Lord's Prayer. Jo says, 'Our Father who art in heaven … ' and then dies.

It is a poignant and lyrical moment in the novel. The religious doctor tries to save also the soul of this vagrant, who does not know Christ because nobody had really talked to him of Him. Once Jo had met an Anglican clergyman who told him sternly that he must not sin. But Jo had not understood anything of that talk, the priest had not realised that the boy simply did not know anything of Jesus. Woodcourt, the doctor, is concerned for the fate of that soul, not just for his physical survival, and tries to save him *in extremis* with the prayer that the Lord taught us.

This is the sort of charity that moves us to tears.

EPILOGUE

June 25, 2022

Your Eminence, many things have happened on a global scale since our last interview: from the developments of the pandemic, to the conflict in Ukraine and the threat of a new Cold War, and much more. But it is on what is happening in the Church that I would like to ask you about. Taking my cue from news that I just saw: recently in Rome the Pontifical University of Saint Anthony, that is the highest institution of theological and canonical study of the Franciscans, held a conference on the theme 'Refuse produces waste: waste management and the common good', with a round table titled 'Refuse, waste and scrap in [the] environmentalist visions towards an integral ecology. Is ecology a new sacred science?'

I WOULD NOT SAY that ecology is a 'new sacred science'. At most, one can speak of an 'ecological ethic' as a new branch of moral theology or ethics. Moral theology studies ethical issues primarily from the perspective of Revelation and Tradition and the teachings of the Church. Ethics does so primarily from a philosophical perspective. In practice, the two complement each other. Philosophical ethics is an auxiliary science for moral theology, of which it makes frequent grateful use. Indeed, Catholic moral theology often chooses the moral natural law as its starting point to assess the moral good or evil of human actions. The moral natural law, which derives from the human creature structure, is based on God's creative order. It applies not only to Catholics, but to all human beings. Every human being can, in principle, know the moral natural law, but this is made more difficult by original sin, which weakens man's will to do good, makes the moral natural law less readily known to our reason, and causes us to be less able to attune our emotional life to what our reason presents as good. Therefore, we are all characterized by an innate selfishness. In order to help us know the moral natural law and thereby put it into practice, God has revealed the moral natural law in the Holy Scriptures, for example in the Ten Commandments. The Holy Spirit is at work in the Tradition of the Church and in a special way enlightens the Church's Magisterium. By reflecting on natural law, revelation, Tradition, and the statements of the Church's Magisterium, ecological ethics can be helpful in discovering and articulating the values and norms that guide our care for the environment. In addition, ecological ethics can be helpful to dispel errone-ous views regarding environmental issues.

Since the 1960s, Christianity has been identified as one of the causes of the current environmental crisis. This is said to be due to Christianity's strong anthropocentrism. God appoints man as steward of creation and thereby makes him ruler of the earth: 'Be fruitful and multiply, and fill the earth and subdue it; and have dominion over the fish of the sea and over the birds of the air and over every living thing that moves upon the earth' (Gen 1:28; cf. Gen 9:2.7; Ps 8). This would have been reinforced by the fact that man on earth is the only creature created in God's image and likeness (Gen 1:26–27). This makes God and his power over creation present. The Hebrew word trans-lated here as 'fill the earth' is meant to mean that man is to occupy the earth as a place to live. However, it can also mean to 'take under one's own wings,' that is, to protect the earth from the chaos or 'formless void' (Gen 1:2) that it is in the beginning. The Hebrew word 'subdue' does not mean that man may exploit or damage the earth, but that he must make it a habitable place for himself, his fellow men, and future generations. The powerful Hebrew term, translated here as 'subdue', must also be read against the background of the announcement that the earth was in the beginning a chaos or a formless void: it is not so easy for man to make it a habitable place. The commission given to man to manage the earth must also be read in conjunction with Gen 2:15: 'The Lord God took the man and put him in the garden of Eden to till it and keep it.' In this there can be no command or permission to exploit the earth. That man was created in God's image and likeness means in every case that he is not God and cannot rule over creation as a God. To 'manage' does not mean that we can do whatever we want with the earth. God appoints us as stewards of creation. As stewards we act on behalf of the owner, and that is God. We are tasked with making the earth a habitable place for the sake of the Common Good, in which not only present but also future generations must share. Through the rapid growth of industry and through our means of transportation, we have polluted the air, the waters and often the soil as well. We will therefore have to switch to new techniques and sources of energy. Moral theologians and ethicists can formulate values and standards for this. However, it is up to politicians to decide how these values are to be realized in practice and how the relevant standards must be applied. Here politicians are dependent on advice from scientists. And in this regard they are faced with the difficulty that scientists do not always give the same advice. For example, climate scientists do not all give the same advice on how to prevent global warming. Some of them even believe that global warming is (partially) a natural development for which humans are not responsible. It would then be a kind of wave motion in the average temperature of the earth over which man has no influence. Politicians are guided by what the majority of climate scientists say. However, theological ethics can only help formulate the values and norms that apply in this field and correct misinterpretations of what the appointment of man as steward of creation entails. However, they lack the expertise to evaluate the theories of climate scientists.

If one looks at the panorama of the pontifical universities, at the production of the theological faculties, even at the interventions of cardinals and theologians that are in vogue, one often has the impression that the doctrine of the faith has become relativized. I am not just speaking of morality, which is just the topic that attracts the most interest today, in fact Christology does not warm the minds nor attract the attention of the newspapers. It is possible to support almost any thesis that does not conform to the Magisterium, without this having any particular consequence. We are asked to be an outgoing Church, but to go out to say what exactly, if internally everything seems to have become fluid and nebulous?

It was the intention of the Second Vatican Council that the Church should open herself to the world. It has been a great disappointment that the world, for its part, has not opened itself to the Church. On the contrary: while the world and the Church largely shared the same values and norms up to and including the Second Vatican Council, the rapid individualization and secularization of society in the second half of the 1960s deeply alienated the Church from the world. An anti-Church attitude even unmistakably developed in Western Europe. The values and norms of society began to differ profoundly from norms and values advocated by the Church's Magisterium. The sexual revolution broke out, people claimed for themselves the right to contraception, free sexual relations outside of marriage that were not aimed at procreation, homosexual acts and later the legalization of marriage between individuals of the same sex. In addition, they also demanded the right to abortion, euthanasia and assisted suicide. The Protestant churches, especially the more liberal ones, adopted many of the views, values and norms of secular society. The Roman Catholic Magisterium, however, remained faithful to the teachings concerning values and norms that have been presented to us in Revelation, by the tradition of the Church, and by the Church Magisterium also in the past. Various moral theologians developed moral theories in the 1960s that could be used to justify the performance of concrete morally evil acts under certain conditions. At first, these theories were used primarily to circumvent the encyclical *Humanae vitae* and to defend the use of contraceptives to prevent pregnancy under certain circumstances. Later, these theories were also applied to justify the performance of other morally evil acts. This, unfortunately, was done by the majority of moral theologians. As a result, Catholic moral theologians adopted in practice a number of secular values and norms

This did not happen only among moral theologians. In the field of the Catholic faith as such, heterodox views came into vogue as well. A number of exegetes who teach and scientifically examine Holy Scripture no longer see in it the revealed Word of God, but regard it as a purely human book. Exegesis thus becomes a kind of ennobled linguistics.

Pope Pius X once said that he had not eradicated Modernism, but suppressed it. He knew that modernists

continued to develop their theories in secret. The mis-
placed expectation that the Second Vatican Council would
also modify the teachings of the Church worked as a
trigger among theologians to develop theories that devi-
ated from Church teaching. They also transferred these
to their students. Those students partly became priests,
deacons or pastoral workers, who used those theories as
a starting point for their preaching and catechesis. Some
of the priests among them are now bishops or cardinals.
As a result of these developments, even in higher echelons
of the Church we encounter conceptions of faith and
morals that contradict the teachings of the Church.

It is therefore of the utmost importance that Grand
Chancellors of theological faculties only authorize the
appointment of professors and teachers who are truly
religious and adhere to the teachings of the Church.
Bishops must provide teachers in their seminaries who are
faithful to the teachings of the Church. These are the
breeding grounds of future priests, bishops and cardinals.
By ensuring reliable theological teaching and research in
theological faculties and seminaries, we will have good
priests in the future who proclaim the faith in accordance
with the teachings of the Church.

This is an important reason why many Catholics hold
views that are sometimes far from the authentic Catholic
faith. However, it is not the only reason. Catholics live in
a bleak secular and anti-church climate. What the Church
teaches is not infrequently openly ridiculed. The prevailing
culture, the media and public opinion have a great influence on Catholics, against which their already weak faith
is often not resistant.

A member of a parish council once asked the bursar of
the Archdiocese if Cardinal Eijk still really believed that

Jesus was the Son of God who became man for us. When the bursar said yes, he was dumbfounded.

Incidentally, it is an encouraging sign that today's seminarians, even if they follow courses with content that deviates from Church teaching, are themselves very pious and faithful to the Church. However, even if they will not adopt the wrong things that are presented to them, a problem remains that part of the Church's teaching that should have been presented to them is withheld.

What does synodality mean to you?

Synodality is derived from two Greek words: 'sun' meaning 'with' or 'together with' and 'hodos', 'way'. Synodality means 'one common way'. In a synodal Church, all members walk one common path. This way is in fact a Person, Jesus Christ, as He says of Himself, 'I am the way, and the truth, and the life' (Jn 14:6).

What connection do you have with the Psalms? It strikes me how the Liturgy of the Hours, the collective prayer of the Church—and the one that every priest has the obligation to recite—still uses these compositions which are so vibrant, pugnacious, with a language and images that are the opposite of the 'ecclesiastically correct' thinking which is in force today. They seem like words from another religion.

The psalms—like the other Old Testament writings—are inspired by the Holy Spirit. Sometimes certain parts of psalms can make a strange impression on us, for example: 'But God will shatter the heads of his enemies' (Ps 68:21). How does this psalm verse relate to the fact that Jesus says to love even your enemies? In interpreting this psalm verse, we must remember that although the texts of the Holy Scripture are inspired by the Holy Spirit, they are also written by human beings so these texts also contain human elements. In this case, these elements come from the poet of the psalm and relate to a historical event that we do not know the details of or cannot interpret at all. However, the original historical context is irrelevant when praying the psalm. The real meaning of the psalms as we pray them in the Liturgy of the Hours can only be understood from the perspective of Christ.

The Church, the mystical Body of Christ, of which we are the members, prays the psalms in the tides together with Christ the head. We do so in the power of that same Holy Spirit who also inspired the poets of the psalms. As we pray the psalms together with Christ and the whole Church, we see how we can place the personal feelings we have in praying psalms. The Holy Spirit makes us understand the psalms from the perspective of Christ. The Old Testament is fulfilled in the New Testament. Among other things, the Church Fathers saw the psalms as a prophecy of what Christ would do for us. They infer this, for example, from what Jesus says to the Emmaus disciples, 'Then beginning with Moses and all the prophets, he interpreted to them the things about himself in all the scriptures' (Lk 24:27). We generally address our psalm prayers together with Christ to God the Father. Jesus already did this during his earthly life together with his disciples. He usually went to the synagogue on Sabbath, where He prayed the psalms with them. He also did this when celebrating the Jewish home liturgy.

We can also understand the meaning of the psalms for our personal lives only through Christ. For example, there are psalms in which the one who prays them presents his needs to God. This is first and foremost the prayer of Christ who addresses the Father in his suffering: 'Your wrath lies heavy upon me, and you overwhelm me with all your waves. You have caused my companions to shun me; you have made me a thing of horror to them. I am shut in so that I cannot escape; my eye grows dim through sorrow. Every day I call on you, O Lord; I spread out my hands to you' (Ps 88, 8–9). By 'Your wrath lies heavy upon me' Christ is referring to our indebtedness that God has placed on His shoulders and that He pays out for us in His death on the Cross. We can let our personal suffering through illness and adversity of any kind be absorbed into the suffering of Jesus and thus into his prayer by praying this psalm.

With the above verse from Psalm 68, which says 'But God will shatter the heads of his enemies' (Ps 68:21), the word enemies refers, for example, to the devil whom Jesus defeated through His death on the Cross and resurrection. But it is also an invitation to ask ourselves to what extent we ourselves are enemies of God. We must remember that all people (except the Virgin Mary) are responsible for Jesus' death on the Cross. This is not a reason for despair. On the contrary. After all, Jesus atoned for our burden of sin on the Cross and thus obtained forgiveness for us. Through His death on the Cross and His resurrection He conquered death. We can only partake of this, however, if we repent of our evil acts, like the good murderer who was crucified at the same time as Jesus along with another murderer: 'And we indeed have been condemned justly, for we are getting what we deserve for our deeds, but this man has done nothing wrong. Then he said, "Jesus, remember me when you come into your kingdom." He replied, "Truly I tell you, today you will be with me in Paradise"' (Lk 23:41–43). Someone who definitively wants to remain an enemy of God is not crushed, but must accept that he will then end up in a condition, hell, in which there is no longer any possibility of seeing God face to face. However, this is ultimately the person's own choice.

Some psalms we pray to Christ: for example, the psalms in which we declare that we are sinners and ask for forgiveness. Of course, Christ cannot say that of Himself. That is, for example, Ps 51, which—historically speaking—David is said to have composed when the prophet Nathan came to him to berate him about his sexual relationship with Bathsheba, the wife of Uriah the Hittite (2 Sam 11:27–12:15): 'Have mercy on me, O God, according to your steadfast love; according to your abundant mercy; blot out my transgressions. Wash me thoroughly from my iniquity, and cleanse me from my sin. For I know my transgressions, and my sin is ever before me. Against you, you alone, have I sinned, and done what is evil in your sight, so that you are justified in your sentence and blameless when you pass judgment. Indeed, I was born guilty, a sinner when my mother conceived me' (Ps 51,15).

There are also psalms in which the Church, together with Jesus, her head, submits what she has to endure to the Father: '"Often have they attacked me from my youth"—let Israel now say—"often have they attacked me from my youth, yet they have not prevailed against me. The ploughmen ploughed on my back; they made their furrows long." The LORD is righteous; he has cut the cords of the wicked. May all who hate Zion be put to shame and turned backward. Let them be like the grass on the housetops that withers before it grows up, with which reapers do not fill their hands or binders of sheaves their arms, while those who pass by do not say, "The blessing of the LORD be upon you! We bless you in the name of the Lord!"' (Ps 129). In the Old Testament, Israel prays the Lord to protect it. From a New Testament perspective, this prayer relates to the Church.

If you were asked to highlight three urgent measures to be taken for the universal Church, what would you say?

To me, three measures for the universal Church seem urgent:

1. In the first place, it is necessary that bishops be appointed who are faithful to the teachings of the Church, and that they can articulate those well in preaching and catechesis. They should also have the administrative capacities to lead Vicars General, other Vicars and collaborators and the clergy in the parishes in such a way that all of them also proclaim and celebrate the faith according to the teachings of the Church. The bishops to be appointed must have integrity, justice, prudence and be of impeccable conduct. If a bishop himself lacks orthodoxy and integrity, there is a good chance that he will appoint associates who are also lacking in orthodoxy and integrity. The reason is that the bishop is the principle of unity of faith in the private church, the diocese, as the pope is to the whole Church. An orthodox bishop who is in control of his diocese administratively appoints rectors and professors of seminaries who, like him, are orthodox and of integrity and people of prayer. If he is grand chancellor, then an orthodox bishop will only give a canonical mission or a permit to teach to professors and teachers who are faithful to the teachings of the Church. This is an important condition for the reliable teaching of the young priests of the future, introducing them to the authentic teachings of the Church and increasing the likelihood that they will transmit them to those who will later be entrusted to their pastoral care. A reliable proclamation in accordance with the teachings of Christ and the Gospel, as propagated by the Church, begins with the bishop. A bishop who himself has integrity will try to avoid scandals in his diocese

and—if they occur—will try to deal with them adequately and justly, and will not give the guilty a backseat, but will ensure that they do not escape their just punishment and will impose on them the necessary measures to prevent recurrence.

2. Secondly, what is urgently needed at this time is an encyclical from the Pope on gender issues. Gender theory is currently rapidly being presented in educational programs in schools under pressure from international organizations. Children are urged to think at the earliest possible age about the gender identity they want to choose later: whether they want to be homosexual, bisexual, transsexual, transgender or non-binary. A transgender person is a transsexual who is considering changing their sexual characteristics—as far as possible—to those of the opposite sex by medical treatment with hormones or by surgery, or who has already done so. In an increasing number of countries it is made possible by law to change gender in civil status records and passports. To children who are unsure of which gender identity to choose, the administration of hormones can delay the onset of puberty. These are hormones that can have serious side effects. The idea is that if the person concerned later wants to have their gender changed physically as well, the necessary treatment can be applied as early as possible, whereby one hopes to achieve the best results. In addition to the gender theory, there is also the queer theory. This holds that gender has no established patterns, but that there are fluid lines between genders. For example, there are not a few young people who sometimes live as heterosexuals and then again as homosexuals or lesbians, thus alternating between different gender identities.

Gender is the social role of men and women. Gender refers to the biological sex. The gender theory and the queer theory are based on the idea that gender and biological sex can be completely disconnected. Of course, the gender, the social role of women can undergo changes over time as a result of cultural changes: it is not written in the biological sex of the woman that she could not have a technical profession, be a professional footballer or a CEO. However, the Church teaches that there is an essential connection between gender and biological sex. Only the woman can be mother, daughter or wife. Just as the man can only be father, son and husband. If this were to be abandoned then it becomes also difficult to proclaim God who has revealed himself as the Father, or God the Son who became man for us. Also, the relationship between Christ and His Church as that of bridegroom and bride would no longer be understood. This would eliminate, for example, the basis for the theology of ministry which says that only a man can represent Christ in person as a priest. How then can Mary still be interpreted as the bride of the Holy Spirit? In short, the passage of the gender theory and the queer theory would make it effectively impossible to proclaim the Christian faith.

For this reason, it is more necessary than ever for a papal encyclical to appear that clearly lays out the essential link between gender and biological sexuality.

3. It is very urgent that innovative pastoral projects with (re)evangelisation as their goal are introduced in our parishes. By this I mean special programmes aimed at acquainting especially younger people and children with Christ and His Gospel. Our parishes—certainly in Western Europe—are, with few exceptions, dying. In the time that I have been Archbishop of Utrecht, namely since 2008, the number of first communicants and confirmands has more than halved. This is not because I am such a terrible Archbishop. It is a development that is visible in

all dioceses in the Netherlands and beyond. Eventually we will face a situation where the flow of first communicants and confirmands will dry up almost completely. At the same time we see that the first communicants, confirmands and their parents are much more serious in their faith. We must take advantage of this. Several of these innovative pastoral projects were suggested by the Canadian priest James Mallon. One of them concerns family Sundays. On a family Sunday, catechesis is given to children and young people of various ages as well as their parents, the Eucharist is celebrated together and a common meal takes place. Catechesis for the parents is a dire necessity, for nowadays they know hardly anything about the Christian faith, as catechesis has been sorely neglected for over half a century. It is striking that the negative attitude of parents towards the Church, which was quite common until recently, is hardly ever seen anymore. Usually there is a certain curiosity about what the Church has to offer about Christ and his Gospel. A number of young priests have started these family Sundays. A few dozen to sometimes 50 or 60 parents with their children, who otherwise would not have gone to church on Sunday, hear something about Christ and his Gospel. Often the parents, children and young people are enthusiastic about these gatherings.

In addition, it is good to introduce young people and adults who do not (yet) have started a family to Christ. The Alpha courses offer a first step in this direction. Approximately half of the participants in the Alpha courses go on to live as active Catholics, if they have already been baptized Catholic, or enter the Catholic Church through baptism and/or confirmation. These people often become ardent followers of Christ. No matter how decayed the Church may be, the Holy Spirit continues to work in it and to open people's hearts to Jesus. The Alpha course, however, requires a follow-up and deepening in the form of adult catechesis.

It is also important to set up good marriage courses. In the Archdiocese of Utrecht, in the autumn of 2022, marriage courses will be offered on a regional level. This regional level is chosen because individual parishes often have too few marriage candidates to organise marriage courses on a parish level. This course consists first of all of a very basic catechesis, followed by an explanation of the meaning of marriage and marriage morals using the theology of the body of Pope John Paul II. There are also some evenings where experienced couples talk about the difficulties that marriage can bring, especially in the first years, and how best to deal with those issues. An element that should not be missed in these marriage courses is that the upcoming bridal couples are taught how to pray. Often they can hardly do this because no one has ever taught them how. The young (future) parents should also know how to raise their children in faith. It is crucial for the future of the Church that young people who are about to marry are introduced to the Christian faith, the Christian views on marriage and family and the life of prayer in this way. For it is they who pass on the Christian faith to their children in the first place.

For young people who have grown up in today's hyper-individualistic culture, it is not easy to live up to the essence of marriage, a total mutual self-giving. In practice, young people run into all kinds of problems that can make their marriage difficult or even undermine it. That is why it is necessary for the diocese, for example, to set up weekends for newlyweds and young families, during which the Eucharist is celebrated, prayers are said together, Christ is proclaimed, and experienced married couples help newlyweds to deal adequately with the problems they encounter in their marriage.

In the last canonizations there was a Dutch footprint: not only was the figure of the Dutch Carmelite Titus Brandsma (1881–1942) canonized, but also the Indian Lazarus Devasahayam Pillai (1712–1752), who came to the faith thanks to the friendship with a Dutch naval officer, Eustachius Benedictus de Lannoy. Will Holland still give us saints? Do you know any living examples?

Cardinal Alfrink opened a beatification process of Mgr Alphons Ariëns in the late 1950s. Alphons Ariëns (1860–1928) was a priest of the Archdiocese of Utrecht). As a seminarian, he attended lectures on church history at the Major Seminary by the priest Herman Schaepman, who had been elected to the Lower House at the time. The latter discussed current political issues with his students and read them the speeches he made in the chamber. His pursuit of the full emancipation of Catholics in the scientific, social and political fields was appreciated by his students, including Alphons Ariëns. After his ordination to the priesthood, the Archbishop, because of his giftedness, allowed Ariëns to continue his studies in Rome at the University of St. Thomas Aquinas (the University of the Dominicans), where he obtained a doctorate in theology. There he developed, also through his international experience, into a courageous man with the necessary entrepreneurial spirit that would later characterize him so much. In Italy he also became acquainted with Franciscan spirituality, which places so much emphasis on personally experienced poverty as an inner virtue. At the Basilica of Portiuncula in Assisi, he had himself clothed as a member of the Third Order of St. Francis. In Italy he also made the acquaintance of St. Don Bosco, then already a very old man, who had in a very meritorious way made the alleviation of the distress of fellow men his life's work. His successors as superior general of the Salesians would later assist Alphons Ariëns in setting up the Catholic Workers Association.

When Alphons Ariëns took office in October 1886 as chaplain to the St. James Parish, a working-class parish in Enschede, the center of the Twente textile industry, he, as a dedicated priest, put his talents in a generous, creative, and enthusiastic way to the service of the largely impoverished population of that factory town, which suffered from unemployment and social problems like widely spread alcoholism. He published numerous articles on social issues, laid the foundations for the Catholic Workers Movement and developed an impressive series of activities to educate workers and to make their lives bearable through proper recreation. Because no miracles have occurred at his intercession, his beatification process cannot be continued up to now.

Another Dutch saint could perhaps be Johannes Cardinal de Jong (1885–1955). He also studied at the Major Seminary of the Archdiocese of Utrecht and became an Archdiocesan priest in 1908. He studied in Rome, too, where he obtained a doctorate in philosophy and one in theology as well. After having performed pastoral work as an assistant priest in Amersfoort, he became professor of church history at the Major Seminary of the Archdiocese of Utrecht in 1914. As such he wrote an important manual on church history. In 1931 he became rector of the seminary, in 1935 followed by his appointment as Coadjutor and a year later as Archbishop of Utrecht. During the Second World War he protested against the Nazi ideology and the deportation of Jews. Together with a Dutch-Reformed pastor, Gravemeijer, he wrote three pulpit messages, two of which were read in Roman-Catholic, Dutch-Reformed and Synodal-Reformed churches. The third one was not read in Dutch-Reformed churches. Archbishop De Jong had in his secret archive a list of hiding addresses of Jewish children and he collected funds to support them. This courageous behaviour was admired by Pope Pius XII, who therefore created him a cardinal in 1946.

Perhaps, the Netherlands could even have had a holy Pope. Pope Adrian VI (the sixth), son of a carpenter, was born on March 2, 1459 in Utrecht as Adriaan Floriszoon Boeyens. For a long time he was a priest and professor at the Catholic University of Leuven. In 1507 he was appointed tutor and teacher to the then seven-year-old Emperor Charles V. In 1515 Charles V appointed him his deputy in Spain, after he had become king of that country. He managed to retain Spain for Charles V. Adrian became bishop of Tortosa in 1516, as well as head of the Spanish government and cardinal. At the end of 1521 he was elected pope at a conclave in which he was not able to take part. On September 31, 1522, he was crowned pope. That was five hundred years ago this year. The Dutch can be proud of Adrian VI. His era is not considered one of the best periods in the history of the Church: there were many abuses. Bishops were mainly political leaders, practically did not care about their pastoral office and often stayed outside their bishoprics. Ecclesiastical offices were traded and mortgaged. The lower clergy was poorly educated, not celibate, and more concerned with fringe piety and eso-teric matters than with preaching the Christian faith.

In the midst of all these developments, Adrian VI was one of the exceptions. He celebrated the Holy Eucharist every day and distinguished himself as a man who loved study and prayer. For this reason he was greatly admired by his contemporaries. Contrary to what was usual, he did not collect well-paid offices, was satisfied with little and gave to the poor what he had left.

Living according to Christian values and principles might be more natural and easier if the whole society propagates these values with conviction. But this was not the case in that age of Adrian VI. In such a situation, what matters is personal spirituality, that is, a lived faith and a living contact with God. These give the strength to swim against the tide. Trust in God is a thread that runs through Adrian's life.

Upon his arrival in Rome, financially he found a smoking pile of rubble left by his predecessor. This Leo X had a well-filled treasury at his disposal, bequeathed to him by his predecessor Julius II, but he was lavish with it especially through his splendorous life. A Venetian envoy estimated the total expenditure during his pontificate at 45 million ducats, currently a huge amount. After his death, people scoffed: 'Never has a pontificate looked so much like the Holy Trinity as that of Leo X. For he brought through the money of three popes: not only his own money, but also that of his predecessor and, from the beginning, of his successor.' For this reason, but also because of his lifestyle, Adrian VI led a conspicuously frugal court. He also demanded this frugality from those around him.

By the way, it must be taken into account that Adrian, even before he arrived in Rome after his appointment, was already known to be an ascetic. He was finally elected pope after a lengthy conclave, which certainly should not be compared with a beauty contest. We would say that his election was the fruit of the action of the Holy Spirit, but from a purely human point of view it was also the result of a politically pathetic compromise. The people of Rome were the least happy about his election. Already the first days after his election, while Adrian did not know what was in store for him (he learned of his election only on January 22, 1522), he was ridiculed in a caricature as a schoolmaster who teaches discipline to cardinals with a rod. Because the memory of Pope Alexander VI, a Spaniard, who, as pope, represented a moral nadir in the history of the papacy was still fresh in one's mind, another pope from Spain, even if he came from the Netherlands, was not considered feasible. There was even talk that he was planning to move the Curia to Spain. In any case, bad guys put up a poster at the Vatican with the notice: 'Palace for rent.' From the beginning—even before his de facto accession—his image was portrayed negatively.

Incidentally, there were also people who reacted positively to his appointment. Among them, of course, was his former pupil Charles V, who hoped to increase his influence on the Holy See and the Papal States through Adrian. But there were also sincere congratulations, among others from Erasmus and the English chancellor Thomas More.

Adrian himself, although outwardly calm and without showing emotion, certainly did not react enthusiastically when he learned of the honour he had received: 'If what I am told is true, I have many reasons to be sad and wistful.' This did not stop him, however, to quickly make a start on the necessary remodelling. While he was still in Saragossa, preparing for the sea voyage to Italy, he already issued new statutes for the papal chancery. One of the most important provisions of the statutes was that the offices were not to be sold, distributed or pledged, which was a common practice at that time. The offices were to be at the disposal of the pope and were to remain so. Moreover, he established a college to deal with the processing of petitions.

Immediately after his arrival in Rome, he received the cardinals in the monastery of St Paul Outside the Walls and received their homage in the sacristy of that church. The dean of the cardinals gave a welcoming speech in which he expressed his expectation that the new pope would begin to implement seven things:

1. Simony and tyranny should be resisted;
2. It was important to implement the reform measures of the Fifth Lateran Council (1512–1517);
3. To guarantee justice to everyone without distinction;
4. To establish a good care for the poor;
5. To seek a truce between the European princes;
6. To prepare a crusade against the advancing Turks;
7. Finally, to accelerate the reconstruction of St. Peter's Basilica.

Adrian took these opinions to heart. In fact, even without this welcoming speech, he would have taken care of these problems. Immediately after his arrival he took a number of measures—not mentioned by the Dean of the Sacred College—concerning the Cardinals. They were deprived of the right of asylum, namely the right to hide criminals; they were no longer allowed to carry weapons; at the same time they had to shave their beards because they looked more like soldiers than priests. But it did not stop there: already on the first day after his papal coronation Adrian addressed an urgent request to the cardinals to send away unworthy persons from their environment, to live in celibacy and to be satisfied with an income of not more than 6000 ducats per year. They were to set a good example to the lower clergy, to devote themselves to study and to assist the pope in carrying out the reform measures to improve the state of the Church. The Rota was forbidden to refuse 'rights' any longer.

We must note, by the way, that Adrian was not very gentle in the reorganization of the College of Cardinals and perhaps did not show enough tact. The cardinals who lived in the Vatican were to leave immediately, except for the Swiss Cardinal Matthäus Schiner, who supported his reform plans. A cardinal with a questionable lifestyle was even denied access to Pope Adrian. Cardinal Giulio de Medici was no longer given precedence, although he had worked hard for his election as pope during the conclave.

Adrian was Pope for too short a time to be able to realize what was in front of his eyes. In the process, he was confronted with huge problems: The political controversies between the Christian princes in Europe, of which he was in danger of becoming the pawn, the advance of the Turks in Eastern Europe, a plague during his reign in Rome and the beginning of the Reformation.

The three great monarchs in Western Europe were Charles V, Emperor of Germany and King of Spain, Francis I, King of France, and the English King Henry VIII. Each of these three turned their eager eyes to Italy, because of its strategic, central position in the Mediterranean. Political negotiators on behalf of Charles V still considered Adrian his subject and assumed that he owed him his election as pope. Adrian, however, maintained his policy of strict neutrality and urged them to make peace among themselves. He considered this a matter of the utmost importance, not only because he himself was a peaceable man, but also because only if they marched together the Christian powers could stand up to the Turks. The Turks had been advancing further into Europe since the fall of Constantinople and thus of the Eastern Roman Empire in 1453. The Balkans had fallen into their hands, they advanced into Hungary and conquered Rhodes, which directly threatened Italy.

Turks had thrown corpses of plague patients into Venetian fortresses. As a result, this contagious disease spread once again across Europe, and in early September 1522 the plague broke out in Rome as well. Cardinals and employees of the Curia fled. Many inhabitants of Rome died of the disease, which did not subside until the beginning of December, when winter set in. Adrian remained at his post with great trust in God. Administratively, however, he was seriously affected for four months. We must be aware that this period covered one third of his whole pontificate.

A huge problem for Adrian VI was, of course, the emerging Reformation, which officially began in 1517. In the fifteenth century, however, one can already see the foreshadowing of this development. In addition to the anger about the customs in the Church, the scholastic theology was increasingly criticized. The University of Louvain was still a bastion of scholasticism at the time when Adrian was lecturing there. Adrian also was a moral theologian in the scholastic tradition. Here we must take into account that the Renaissance showed much more interest in the subject and his personal relationship with Christ. This in itself valuable development, which we see again very clearly, for example, in the movement of the so-called Modern Devotion in the Netherlands, would, however, develop in the sixteenth century in such an extreme way that the role of the Church as an institute was only secondarily acknowledged with regard to the beginning and maintenance of a personal relationship with Christ. This attitude is also found in Protestant ecclesiology.

The Reformation arose in the last years of the pontificate of Leo X, who—already afflicted with the tendency to take things less seriously—saw in Luther nothing more than a rebellious monk. Adrian had other thoughts about it, but he saw his appearance in the first place as a protest against the circumstances in the Church. Therefore, he assumed that the internal renewal of the Church, which would eradicate these grievances, would of itself lead to the reformers returning to the Mother Church. He had misjudged this, but it brought him to a unique act. He was the first pope to pronounce a *Mea Culpa* (through my fault) because of the circumstances in the Church. This *Mea Culpa* can be found, along with a rejection of Luther's doctrine, in an instruction read by his legate Francesco Chieregati in the Empire Day of Worms on January 3, 1523, in which Adrian admitted that God allowed the persecution of the Church because of the sins of men, especially priests and prelates, especially in spiritual matters. He had the courage to also put the blame on himself: 'We know that even in the Holy See for many years there have been reprehensible things, abuses in spiritual matters and transgressions of the command-ments, indeed that everything has become a nuisance. Therefore, it is not surprising that the disease has passed from the head to the members or, more specifically, from the pope to the prelates.'

To this *Mea Culpa* he attached the promise to put an end to the circumstances. He also promised that contro-versial processes of the Rota would be re-examined. We have become somewhat accustomed to papal *Mea Culpas* because John Paul II did it a few times. But 427 years before John Paul II did it, it was an absolute novelty. With the *Mea Culpa* and the promises it brought, Adrian hoped to keep the Reformation in check. The desired success, however, failed to materialize. The prelates present felt insulted and were not willing to cooperate. The Lutherans did not trust his *Mea Culpa*.

During his life, Adrian VI, despite his good intentions, was not able to realize the restoration of the Church. He was pope for too short a time, only one year and two weeks. He died on September 14, 1523. Erasmus, who—though having sincerely congratulated Adrian on his election as pope—was initially critical of his pontificate, later thought that Adrian could have succeeded at least in the transformation of the clergy if he had lived only ten years longer. His pontificate, however, lasted much too short to solve the huge problem he faced. Are we therefore forced to conclude that his pontificate was actually unsuccessful? Adrian's biographers give this impression, and the same can be said of his epitaph:

> *Proh dolor, quantum refert in quae tempora vel optimi cuiusq(ue) virtus incidat.*

In English this can be rendered: 'Ah, it makes a great difference in which time the merits of even the best man fall'. I myself think that his pontificate should not be qualified as a success. The success of Jesus during His earthly life was not great either and that life ended with what can only be qualified in human eyes as a catastrophe: His death on the Cross. But its fruit was the resurrection, our salvation, the outpouring of the Holy Spirit, the Church that spread in a short time. From this point of view of the Christian faith, it is not the successes that count, but the fruits. And Adrian's commitment and that of his companions bore fruit very abundantly later in the sixteenth century. In the twenties of that century the time was not yet ripe for a counter-reformation. The awareness that many things were going badly in the Church was already there, but it still had to mature. The need for a radical transformation was not yet felt. The willpower to improve things was still too much lacking among cardinals, bishops and prelates. But Adrian certainly helped to lay the seed for the restoration that would probably come about later in the same century. As stated above, it is known that on the day after his papal coronation Adrian made additional demands to the cardinals. On the occasion of this event, a lively discussion took place among them: such demands had not been presented to the cardinals by a pope for a long time. The radical and manifest improvement was started in the second half of this century, with the help of the Council of Trent. The Church has a divine and a human side. Human beings can fail, but thanks to the guidance of the Holy Spirit, the Church also has a great self-purifying capacity. It is very important to always believe in it, even if you do not see the results of your work immediately.

Adrian remained a believer in this. In the midst of all these circumstances, Adrian VI remained himself: a priest who was faithful to his vocation, body and soul, trusting in the promise that Jesus made to the first Pope: 'You are Peter, and on this rock I will build My Church, and the gates of hell shall not prevail against it' (Mt 16,18). His fidelity to the Church cost him dearly: he was met with failure and abuse. He himself saw the tiara as a heavy burden, which he nevertheless took upon himself because he considered it to be God's will. '*Patere et sustine,*' namely 'be patient and persevere,' was his motto for a reason. Even if God's answer to the prayer of many for the rebuilding of the Church seemed not forthcoming, Adrian remained confident that it would surely come and that it would not come too late (cf. Hab 2:2–4).

Pope Adrian VI remains a source of inspiration for our time, the first quarter of the twenty-first century, as well. We are living anew a time that is in some respects extremely difficult for the Church. The number of priests and religious in Western Europe has decreased sharply since the sixties. Church attendance is low. Many churches are withdrawn from worship and closed. In many parish churches, people older than sixty are by far in the majority. Religious vibrancy is a rarity among Christians in Western Europe at the moment. Even in our age, unfortunately, there are abuses in the Church. What has recently come to light about sexual abuse of minors by priests and religious has damaged the image of the Church in no small measure. For all this, a sincere *Mea Culpa* is in order. Pope Benedict XVI asked God and the people involved for forgiveness for abuse of minors by priests in his homily during the Eucharistic celebration in St. Peter's Square on the High Feast of the Sacred Heart on June 11 2010, on the occasion of the conclusion of the Year for Priests.

What will be the situation in the Church in the second half of this century, many worried faithful ask themselves. In this regard, Pope Adrian VI is an undeniable source of inspiration and encouragement to us. Even if we do not yet see the reconstruction of the Church in our lives, we should nevertheless patiently persevere and stand firm with the same confidence that Adrian VI had in the promise that God watches over his Church. For us, too, his motto has undiminished validity: '*Patere et sustine*': 'Be patient and persevere.'

www.ingramcontent.com/pod-product-compliance
Lightning Source LLC
Chambersburg PA
CBHW022026090426
42739CB00006BA/303